Sticky Bible Skits

20 comical skits
for children's ministry

from the **Skitguys**

Tommy

Eddie

Group
Real. **Bold.** *Love.*

Group resources really work!

This Group resource incorporates our R.E.A.L. approach to ministry. It reinforces a growing friendship with Jesus, encourages long-term learning, and results in life transformation, because it's

Relational
Learner-to-learner interaction enhances learning and builds Christian friendships.

Experiential
What learners experience through discussion and action sticks with them up to 9 times longer than what they simply hear or read.

Applicable
The aim of Christian education is to equip learners to be both hearers and doers of God's Word.

Learner-based
Learners understand and retain more when the learning process takes into consideration how they learn best.

Group

Sticky Bible Skits: 20 Comical Skits for Children's Ministry
Copyright © 2015 The Skit Guys

Visit our website: **group.com**

Credits
Authors: Eddie Woodard and Tommy James
Editors: Christine Yount Jones, Jennifer Hooks, Cindy Hansen, and Lyndsay Gerwing
Chief Creative Officer: Joani Schultz
Cover Design: Sheila Reinhart
Interior Design: Rebecca Swain and Randy Kady
Photos: © istock.com

ISBN: 978-1-4707-1885-5
Printed in the United States of America.
10 9 8 7 6 5 4 3   25 24 23 22 21 20 19 18

TaBLe of contents

Introduction to Sticky Skits

What's a Sticky Skit?

When we think about the word *sticky* in conjunction with kids, we tend to get worried. I mean, let's be honest: Sticky and kids are usually a bad combination. The concept conjures up images of little Timmy Torkelson after downing half a dozen peanut-butter-and-honey sandwiches. Or you may be picturing Susie Saunders reaching for your precious heirloom Bible right after she devoured a swirl of cotton candy that was half her size. And yet these two little examples of *sticky* are exactly what we were thinking about when we came up with the idea of *Sticky Bible Skits.*

But today we want to introduce a new way to think about *sticky* as it relates to kids.

We've crafted 20 humorous and engaging skits that'll stick with kids long after they leave your class or group setting. We hope to provide you with skits that'll feed kids' souls and leave them sticky with the lessons, messages, and guidance of the Bible dripping off them.

Will This Be Sticky for Me to Do?

Yes. No. Maybe? Here's what we mean by that: The skits in this book are arranged in biblical order. So if you're someone who's looking for a companion skit to go along with your Bible passage and you plan ahead, then simply find the script that coincides with your teaching lesson.

But maybe you just need a skit for fun, to perform in "big church," or as a last-minute time filler. In that case, to let you know how much preparation is necessary in regards to the complexity of preparing and performing each skit, we will speak to you in the classic language you no doubt already speak: coffee.

(We call it "classic" to make you think it's been around for years. However, we just made it up. Literally. Just now.)

The "Classic" Coffee Method:

Each skit has been rated for difficulty based on props needed, the preparation needed to get it ready, and the difficulty of memorizing the script. Each skit falls into one of three categories of difficulty: Instant, Almost Instant, or Percolator.

INSTANT When your morning is short but your need is great, you turn to instant coffee to save the day. Similarly, when you find yourself needing a skit in a pinch, this is the kind of skit for you. Preparation time is almost nonexistent. The props needed, if any, can be found in almost any church setting. There's either no memorization needed or the actors can simply hold the script during the performance. These skits are perfect for when you have a skit emergency or just want to do something spontaneous and fun with your kids.

ALMOST INSTANT The greatest man-made invention in the history of earth is the single-cup coffee brewing system. (We read that on the Internet, so it has to be true.) While almost-instant coffee takes a little longer than instant, it's worth the work to get something a little better tasting. Likewise, an Almost Instant skit will take you about an hour in terms of props and preparation. The scripts have been written so there's little memorization or you can use the script during the performance. The more time you choose to put into these skits, the better they'll be. Even so, you can put them together pretty quickly if needed.

PERCOLATOR Grandma made the best coffee. (At least that's what we thought until we discovered $2-per-cup coffee with free Wi-Fi! *It's a router, Grandma, not a magic box. Get with the times!)* Brewed coffee takes time, but the taste is worth it. And so are our Percolator skits. They're a little longer, the props are more thorough, and the scripts ask more of your actors in terms of memorization. However, the results pay off. These are the skits you may decide to perform for the entire church. (And sell $2 coffee to raise money for kids' camp!)

As you look through the book, you'll notice one of these descriptors next to each script. This descriptor will help you find the perfect type of skit for your specific need.

Sticky Is Good!

The best foods are sticky: candied apples, cotton candy, and s'mores! By that same token, we think the best skits should be sticky for kids. We've worked hard to create ideas and actions that'll stick with your kids. It may be a funny line or two, it could be the creative group involvement, or it could even be a prop. Whatever the case, these skits will be engaging and memorable. So have fun, and if you get a chance, send us an email or a tweet to let us know how you used *Sticky Bible Skits.*

Tommy & Eddie
The Skit Guys

www.skitguys.com
@skitguys

Total Ambush Makeover

Purpose: The Creation events are told from the perspective of two besties: Heaven and Earth. These two friends explain that although we may not understand God's design or process, his purpose for us is to be a beautiful masterpiece. God can take what we perceive to be "nothing" and make us into a creation of his design.

Passage: Genesis 1:1–2:2

People: 2 females—Heaven, Earth

Props:
- flashlights (1 per person)
- spray bottles filled with water (1 per person)
- cotton balls (1 per person)
- kazoos (1 per person)
- paper (1 sheet per person)
- 3 copies of the skit

Prep: Ask one child to man the light switch. Give the child a copy of the skit so he or she can follow the prompts.

Give each child in the audience one of each prop—flashlight, spray bottle, cotton ball, kazoo, and sheet of paper.

Give Heaven and Earth the props as well. They'll guide the audience participation throughout the skit. They can use the flashlights to read the scripts when the lights are out.

Choose two females to play the characters of Heaven and Earth. Have them use "valley girl" accents. (You know, like, those girls who, like, use the word *like* totally way too many, like, times in a conversation.) Also, they both, like, use their hands, like…Totally. A. Lot.

Note to Director: Have the actors memorize the script, or (to keep this skit to an Almost Instant) print copies of the skit, put each copy in a binder, and place the binders on music stands. The actors can read their lines like "readers theater."

(LIGHTS DIM)

Heaven: Hello, my name's Heaven. And this is my friend, Earth. *(Gestures with both hands to Earth.)*

Earth: *(Hugs Heaven.)* We're, like, best friends forever. Like, literally. And we have an amazing story to tell about our first adventure together!

Heaven: *(Hugs Earth.)* Okay, so it all started a really, really, really long time ago. Earth came totally out of nowhere.

Earth: For real. God created me, and I was all, like *(slumps shoulders)*, dark and awkward.

Heaven: *(Nods head.)* She totally was. And then all of a sudden we both started hearing God's voice. And Earth started to change!

Earth: *(Excitedly jumps up and down.)* It's like every time God spoke, something totally radical started happening to me! Little did I know, I was getting a total ambush makeover!

Heaven: So awesome! God started with light. It was like he flipped this huge switch or something! *(Motions as if turning on a light switch.)*

(LIGHTS ON)

Earth: We were all, "No way!" because it totally changed everything. God called it "day." We called it "fabulous"! *(Gives Heaven a high five.)*

Heaven: It lasted a while, but then it, like, got all dark again!

(LIGHTS OFF)

Heaven: We were a little freaked out! *(Huddles close to Earth.)* But God was all, "Hey, I'll make it dark at night so you can rest. It'll shine again tomorrow because I have more to do. Relax!" *(Heaven and Earth relax.)*

(LIGHTS ON)

Earth: *(Perks up.)* God was so not kidding about having more to do! He created this cool space and gave me a whole new dimension called "sky." God added these cute little puffy white things, and it totally took me from "drab" to "fab"! *(Throws cotton ball in the air and motions for audience to join in.)*

Heaven: Oh yes it did! Then the swirling started…The sea and the land separated. And because God knows, like, everything, he knew that blue and brown perfectly complement one another. The blue sea next to the brown earth… simply stunning! *(Squirts spray bottle and motions for audience to join in.)*

Earth: And God was just getting started with all the colors. *(Motions for everyone to set the spray bottles down.)* Next, God started bedazzling me with all this green stuff. *(Looks at hands and feet.)*

Heaven: I remember how I was all, like, "Gross me out! *(Points to Earth.)* You have a nasty rash!" But God was all like "I meant to do that" and he called the green stuff plants and trees.

Earth: So I chilled out. *(Looks relaxed.)*

(LIGHTS OUT)

Earth: I was kinda glad when it got dark again because I totally needed to chillax a little.

(LIGHTS ON)

Heaven: *(Perks up.)* Okay, so then the next day was, like, the coolest because God brought out the…

Both: *(Fling fingers wide.)* Bling!

Earth: There was, like, this huge bright light *(motions with one hand up high)* and this smaller glowy one *(motions with other hand up high)*, and God called them "sun" and "moon."

(LIGHTS OFF)

Heaven: But our most favorite were the tiny twinkly ones God called "stars." *(Turns on flashlight and motions for audience to join in.)*

Earth: We could've totally hung out and looked at those stars forever because they were so pretty and there were so many!

(LIGHTS ON)

Earth: But the sun came out again, and then it got really bizarre! *(Motions for everyone to turn off the flashlights and set them down.)* I felt this tickling all over, and these, like, flappy things were moving all up in my face! *(Flaps sheet of paper in the air and motions for audience to join in.)*

Total Ambush Makeover

Heaven: Fish and birds. They were super beautiful and made Earth look really pretty and all. But what happened next was *not* exactly beautiful. These totally weird sounds started coming out of her. I was all like "You totally shouldn't be doing that in public!" *(Holds nose with thumb and forefinger. Then sets down the paper, hums into the kazoo, and motions for audience to join in.)*

Earth: I promise, it wasn't me! It was about a bazillion kinds of animals all running around making noises! And then we realized something else. *(Leads everyone in putting down the kazoos.)*

Heaven: God is, like, the total best at accessorizing! You can't imagine *(places hands on both sides of head)* all the different kinds of creatures God made for Earth. But just when we thought it couldn't get any better…

Earth: There was the big reveal. *(Spreads arms wide.)* God totally saved the best for last. It was like God took a selfie and used it to create these beautiful creatures he called "humans." Their job was to take care of each other and take care of me! *(Earth and Heaven go out to audience and hug several people and then motion for kids to hug each other.)*

Heaven: *(Spreads arms wide.)* Humans were the most incredible things we'd ever seen. And God gave them everything they needed to eat, like this fantastic all-you-can-eat, organic buffet. God thought of everything!

Heaven: *(Nods head.)* Yes. When God made me *(places both hands on chest)* and when he made people *(points to audience)*, God thought of every detail. God totally loved it when all of his creation was finished.

Heaven: *(Turns to face Earth.)* I'm so glad God made you, bestie! *(Hugs Earth.)*

Earth: *(Hugs Heaven.)* Me too, bestie. *(Motions to audience.)* I'm so glad God made you too.

Both: We're so glad God made everything—and God made everything good! *(Give a thumbs-up.)*

sticky Talk

Use these discussion points with your group following the skit.

1. Explain whether you think creation was more like a Disney movie with lights and magic or more like an old man sitting over a potter's wheel—and why. What do you imagine creation sounded and smelled like?

2. During Creation, every time God spoke, something radical started happening to earth. Explain whether you think God is still speaking. Tell about a time God spoke to you in some way.

3. When we're young, we ask questions like "How big is the sky?" Eventually we learn to understand answers such as "Too big for us to understand." How do you feel knowing that God is bigger than we can understand? What clues do you see in the world to show how big and amazing God truly is?

4. If human beings are God's selfies, explain whether you think God is smiling. Tell whether you think God is more likely to press "delete" or "share" when looking at his creation today—and why.

5. The Bible says "God rested"—but it doesn't say "God finished." How do you think God is still creating?

Total Ambush Makeover

Liar, Liar, Pants on Fire

Almost **Instant**

Purpose: The fall of man and woman is told by Satan. Satan is full of lies, and we can't trust a single thing he says. He pretends to do "cool tricks," but his only intention is to insult God.

Passage: Genesis 3

People: Satan, Adam, Eve

Props:
- apple
- 1 copy of the skit

Prep: You can play the role of Satan (or ask another volunteer to). Ask a male and female to play the roles of Adam and Eve. Have them sit in the audience until you ask them to join you.

Note to Director: Prior to the skit, tell the kids, "Every time the person playing the role of Satan says 'I promise,' you'll yell 'Liar, liar, pants on fire!' " Practice the response a few times. Then say, " 'Satan' will ask you a few other questions during the skit. Yell out responses at that time as well. It may be a simple 'yes' or 'no.' "

Satan: *(Spreads arms wide.)* Good evening, and welcome to the garden—the Garden of Eden, that is. You can read about it at the beginning of the Bible. *(Takes a deep breath.)* My name is Satan. You may think of me as a no-good trickster. *(Mockingly bows head.)* That I am. *(Proudly stands straight and then blows on fingernails and brushes them against shirt, as if polishing them.)* Tonight I'm going to tell you about my greatest and most famous trick of all time. It's an oldie but a goodie! I call it the "Adam and Eve Super Duper Deceive." Before I tell you all about it, I'm going to need a volunteer...Is there a girl who can come up and help me?

("EVE" WAVES HAND HIGH AND THEN COMES FORWARD.)

Satan: *(Motions to volunteer.)* Now, you'll be Eve. This trick is very simple. All you have to do is take a bite of this fruit. *(Holds up apple.)* Looks tasty, doesn't it? And that's not all! Not only is it deee-lish, but it will turn you into an instant smarty-pants! *(Raises eyebrows and looks at the audience.)* I promise!

Audience: Liar, liar, pants on fire!

Satan: *(Jumps as if reacting to the yelling.)* Okay, now wait a minute. There's no need for yelling and name-calling here! God put all these beautiful trees here in the garden, didn't he? *(Nods head up and down and motions for audience to respond.)*

Audience: Yes!

Satan: So it's totally fine for Eve to eat whatever she wants, right? *(Shakes head side to side and motions for audience to respond.)*

Audience: No!

Satan: Well, anyway...God gave Adam and Eve the whole garden but said *not* to eat the fruit from the tree in the middle of the garden. *(Motions to the apple.)* *This* fruit is from *that* tree. *(Takes an impatient breath.)* But...let's just get on with the "Adam and Eve Super Duper Deceive" trick. *(Gives Eve the apple.)* Go ahead, Eve, take a bite.

(EVE BITES THE APPLE.)

Satan: So Eve took a bite of the fruit and loved it. In fact, she loved it so much that she called Adam to come and taste it too. Who wants to be my next volunteer? I need a boy this time...

("ADAM" WAVES HAND HIGH AND THEN COMES FORWARD.)

Satan: *(Motions to volunteer.)* Thank you so much for helping me out. You'll be Adam. I won't hurt you. *(Raises eyebrows and looks at the audience.)* I promise!

Audience: Liar, liar, pants on fire!

Satan: *(Places hands on hips and looks sternly at the audience.)* Okay, that's starting to annoy me. *(Motions to the volunteers.)* Now, Eve didn't want to be selfish, so she shared the fruit with Adam.

(EVE HANDS THE APPLE TO ADAM, AND HE TAKES A BITE.)

Satan: Well, at least I didn't lie about everything. Taking a bite out of the fruit *did* make Adam and Eve smart, because they both realized they didn't have a stitch of clothing on! So they tried to hide from God. *(Adam and Eve crouch down.)* Well, even though Adam and Eve disobeyed God, God still loved them and covered them with clothing. But Adam and Eve had to leave that gorgeous garden.

(ADAM AND EVE GO SIT BACK DOWN.)

Satan: God told me that because I'd performed my tricks, I was now cursed to crawl on the ground! And it wasn't even my fault! *(Raises eyebrows and looks at audience.)* I promise!

Audience: Liar, liar, pants on fire!

Satan: *(Places hands on hips again and sighs deeply.)* Oh, so you're going to take God's side, I see! Well, if it hadn't been for someone named Jesus who came later, you and I could've still had a great time doing our tricks together. *(Raises eyebrows and looks at audience.)* I promise!

Audience: Liar, liar, pants on fire!

Satan: Ah…forget it! *(Motions with both hands to the audience and exits in a big huff.)*

Liar, Liar, Pants on Fire

Use these discussion points with your group following the skit.

1. Tell about the best place you've ever been to and why it was the best. What was it like for you when you had to leave? Adam and Eve had the best place ever, and then they messed up and broke the rules and had to leave. Explain why you think it can be so hard to follow rules—even when God tells us to follow them.

2. Did you know Satan's name comes from a very old word: *ha-satan*. It means "obstacle." That's like when you're walking down a path and suddenly there's a giant boulder in your way. You have to climb over it or turn back. Tell about a time you thought everything was going fine and suddenly there was a great big boulder in your way.

3. Sometimes it seems like the wrong thing to do is the most fun. Tell about something that seems like fun to you even though you know it's not the right thing to do. What do you think makes that thing seem like the right thing? How do you know in your heart it's the wrong thing?

4. Tell about a time you blamed someone else when you messed up. (We've all done it.) Adam pointed the finger at Eve. Eve blamed the snake. Satan said, "It's not *my* fault." Why do you think people seem to automatically blame someone else when they mess up?

5. Explain why you think God put the apple in the garden in the first place. Why do you think humans tend to do things God doesn't want us to do? What are ways we can focus on doing the things God tells us to do?

Instant

Live From the Red Carpet

Purpose: "Noah's Ark" is told from the perspective of a reporter talking with the animals as they board the ark. Using a different spin on the Bible passage, this skit shows Noah's obedience in completing a project that would've surely made headlines today!

Passage: Genesis 7:1–9:17

People: Reporter

Props:
- microphone (or pretend with a comb or wooden spoon)
- 1 copy of the skit

Prep: You can play the role of the Reporter (or ask another volunteer to). Speak into the microphone (reporter-like) throughout the entire skit. Use the microphone to cue the audience to make animal noises.

Notes to Director: Prior to the skit, have kids practice sounding off as each of these animals: monkeys, elephants, lions, and laughing hyenas. Then practice the skit's ending. Everyone will shout, "God shut the door!" and then clap one time, as if a door is shutting.

Have the Reporter hold the script as if it's reporter notes. The more the person is familiar with the script, the better it will be.

Reporter: (Enters and then faces audience and talks as if looking into a camera.) Good evening, and welcome to our live coverage of the Noah's Ark red carpet event! We've been following Noah as he's built this huge boat on dry land. (Motions behind, toward the ark. Turns around and makes even bigger motion to show the ark is huge and then faces the audience again.) Wow, that's big! Tonight—with rain in the forecast—two of every living creature will make their way to this gigantic vessel. Let's see if we can catch up to some of the animals now. (Looks to the right and left.) Oh, I think I see a couple of elephants approaching… Elephants! Elephants! (Waves arms and takes a couple of steps to the side as if trying to catch the elephants' attention.) Question, please. Everyone wants to know…How do you feel about stepping into the ark tonight? (Holds microphone out and cues audience.)

Audience: (Makes elephant noises.)

Reporter: (Tilts head as if trying to understand the elephants.) Oh. So you say it's a lot better than getting wet for 40 days and 40 nights. I'd not heard that forecast! What other details do you elephants know about the predicted rain? (Holds microphone out and cues audience.)

Audience: (Makes elephant noises.)

Reporter: (Shakes head.) Really? That bad? I've heard of widespread showers, but the entire earth?! Sounds pretty outrageous! Where'd you elephants find out about this boat, and how'd you get invited to climb on board? (Holds microphone out and cues audience.)

Audience: (Makes elephant noises.)

Reporter: (Speaks to elephants.) Oh, you have to go now? Yes, go ahead and make your way inside. I'd try to get a spot on the second floor myself if I were afraid of mice. Thank you for your time! (Jumps to the side as if letting determined elephants through.)

(Faces audience and talks as if looking into a camera.) And that's all we have from the elephant family, folks, but I think I see some other animals swinging by! Maybe they can tell us more. (Nods head up and down and side to side as if watching monkeys swing toward the ark.) Good evening, monkeys! I must say you're looking quite fabulous tonight! Tell our audience at home why you came here for this big event! (Holds microphone out and cues audience.)

Audience: (Makes monkey noises.)

Reporter: (Tilts head as if trying to understand monkeys.) Cupcakes? Noah said there'd be cupcakes on the boat? (Holds microphone out and cues audience.)

Audience: *(Makes monkey noises.)*

Reporter: *(Nods head.)* Yes, in fact, I *have* heard of "monkey on a cupcake"! But before you go in and enjoy those sweet treats, what do you monkeys think you'll see inside of this ginormous boat? *(Holds microphone out and cues audience.)*

Audience: *(Makes monkey noises.)*

Reporter: *(Nods head again.)* Well, I'm sure there'll be lots of places for you monkeys to swing! *(Turns toward ark and waves as if monkeys are boarding; then turns back.)* Those monkeys never fail to entertain. *(Looks to the right and left.)* Hold on, hold on! I think I see some lions making their way toward me now! *(Stands on tiptoes and looks toward back of room. Bows slightly.)* Hello, your highnesses! As kings of the jungle, you must have all the juicy details about tonight's event! *(Holds microphone out and cues audience.)*

Audience: *(Roars like lions.)*

Reporter: *(Jumps as if startled by the loud roar.)* Oh yes. Sorry. I'll try not to use the word *juicy* again. I'm sure it'll be difficult to be close to all these animals without getting hungry. So what's up with Noah building this big boat? Looks like it's built to take quite a journey! *(Holds microphone out and cues audience.)*

Audience: *(Roars like lions.)*

Reporter: *(Speaks to lions.)* Wow. I knew Noah must be a hard worker to build a boat like this, but I had no idea Noah was the most righteous, most faithful man on earth. So, lions, was it Noah's idea to start this enormous project? *(Holds microphone out and cues audience.)*

Audience: *(Roars like lions.)*

Reporter: *(Nods head.)* Noah was obeying God's command, you say? How interesting! Thanks for sharing on your way to the ark. *(Waves to lions as they board the ark, and then faces the camera again.)* As usual, the lions are in the know. Noah and his family must certainly be special. The lions said God was unhappy with the bad things people were doing and decided to flood the whole earth. Many of us thought this was some kind of stunt or joke! *(Looks to the right and left.)* And speaking of jokes, here come the laughing hyenas! *(Waves to hyenas.)* Excuse me, laughing hyenas! Yes, hello…Do you know where I might find Noah? I'd love to speak to the man who hears God's voice! *(Holds microphone out and cues audience.)*

Audience: *(Laughs like laughing hyenas.)*

Live From the Red Carpet

Reporter: *(Tilts head to side as if trying to understand.)* No, I haven't checked to see if the hippos ate Noah. Very funny. Do you always joke around like that? *(Holds microphone out and cues the audience.)*

Audience: *(Laughs like laughing hyenas.)*

Reporter: *(Steps aside as if letting hyenas through.)* I think I'll follow you hyenas on board. I'd like to ask Noah what it feels like to do this huge project and what'll happen to those of us not invited inside. *(Takes a few steps as if trying to follow hyenas. Stands on tiptoes to try to see what's inside the ark. Sighs and then faces audience.)* Well, it's just awfully crowded in that ark. It looks as though the hyenas are the last to make their way inside. *(Turns around to face ark.)* Well, take a look at that! *(Turns back to audience.)* God shut the door! *(Claps.)* Say that with me!

Audience: God shut the door! *(Claps.)*

Reporter: Amazing! *(Takes a deep breath and then shrugs shoulders.)* Well, that's it, folks. All the animals are now inside what appears to be a lifesaving vessel for a big flood headed our way. Tune in for live coverage after the waters recede and we join them again for the exclusive post-flood after-party! Goodbye! *(Waves to audience and then exits.)*

Use these discussion points with your group following the skit.

1. Describe the loudest thunder you've ever heard. Now describe the closest you've been to a lightning strike. Explain whether you think storms are scary or cool, and why. Why do you think we sometimes feel frightened of storms?

2. Imagine you went to sleep tonight and had the most realistic dream you'd ever had in which God told you he wanted you to be a pro golfer. Explain whether you'd wake up and forget about it or go buy a set of clubs and why. What do you think it would take for you to believe such a dream was real?

3. Think about your life right now. What kind of direction do you think God has already given you? What are you building toward in your life right now, and why?

4. The flood was a sort of reset. Think of a time you had to reset your computer, tablet, or phone or a time you crashed a computer. How do you start over when that happens and you lose everything? How can you reset with God when you make a mistake or poor choice?

Abraham Sacrifices Cletus

Purpose: Abraham offers Isaac, as told by a narrator and two confused actors. Kids will see a physical interpretation of God's provision to Abraham.

Passage: Genesis 22:1-18

People: Narrator, Winston, Cletus

Props:
- podium (or music stand)
- table
- spray bottle filled with water
- ball cap
- 3 copies of the skit

Prep: You can play the role of the Narrator (or ask another volunteer to). Ask two other people to be Winston and Cletus, and give them each a copy of the skit. Give Cletus a ball cap to wear backward. Winston is very proper and speaks with a British accent (if possible). Cletus is an enthusiastic, over-the-top, back-woodsy goofball.

Set the podium or music stand to one side of the stage for the Narrator. Place a copy of the skit on it. Set the table just off center opposite the podium. Place the spray bottle near the table.

Note to Director: Instruct the actors to be "over the top" in actions and expressions. More is better in this skit!

Abraham Sacrifices Cletus

Narrator: *(Enters very properly and walks to podium.)* Hello, and welcome to Biblical Theater World. Or as we call it, "BTW." *(Laughs briefly and then regains composure.)* Today we'll present the classic Bible account of Abraham offering his one and only son, Isaac, as a sacrifice to God. Abraham's way of proving that he loves…our… Lord….Or as we say, "LOL." *(Laughs again briefly, impressed with self. Regains composure quickly.)* Today you're in for a treat! We have two of the finest actors in the theater with us. Both are classically trained members of the British Fancy Fellowship. Or as we say, "BFF." *(Starts to laugh again but Winston interrupts.)*

Winston: *(From offstage)* Oh, for crying out loud! That's enough!

Narrator: *(Regains composure quickly. Looks toward Winston's voice.)* Party pooper! *(Looks back at audience.)* Please welcome our actors. *(Looks at script to read names.)* Playing the role of Father Abraham will be Sir Winston Hillchurch. *(Winston enters from offstage, very proper.)* And playing the role of his one and only son, Isaac, will be Sir Anthony Hammerbottom. *(Cletus enters from offstage, very goofball.)*

Narrator: *(Says to Cletus.)* Excuse me, sir. You're not Sir Anthony Hammerbottom.

Cletus: *(Laughs hysterically.)* You said "Hammerbottom"!

Narrator: *(Stands stiff and straight.)* Sir! Manners!

Cletus: *(Stops laughing.)* Oh, sorry! Yeah. Sir Bottomhammer done got sick, so they sent me in.

Narrator: *(Sternly looks at Cletus.)* Are you an actor?

Cletus: *(Shakes head.)* No, I'm a plumber. But they said this thing was gonna go in the toilet without the other guy…so I figured I'd be a good guy to try to fix it.

Narrator: *(Shakes head.)* Hmm. This is highly irregular.

Cletus: *(Stands straight.)* Well, I'm highly irregular, so this oughta work out great.

Narrator: *(Shakes head again.)* Umm…okay. Well, let's get to what happened in the Bible. *(Takes a deep breath.)* Abraham was a faithful man. God knew that Abraham loved him very much. God told Abraham to give him a sacrifice to show his great love and faith in God.

Winston: *(Goes down on one knee and looks to heaven. Uses a big voice and giant hand motions.)* I love God so much. I'll show my love for God by being obedient and making the sacrifice he's called me to make.

Cletus: *(Takes off ball cap and holds it over heart, as if before the national anthem. Speaks to Winston.)* Wow! You're real good at this acting thing, Winny!

Winston: *(Looks sternly at Cletus.)* It's Winston. And you need to stay in character. Call me Abraham. I am your father.

Cletus: *(Smiles at Winston.)* Oh, yeah. I forgot. Sorry, Dad! Hey, since you're my father, can we have a light saber fight? *(Makes light saber noises and acts as if using a saber.)*

Narrator: *(Places pointer finger to lips.)* Shh! Now where was I? Ah yes…*(Takes a deep breath.)* So Abraham agreed to make a great sacrifice to God. He took his son—his only son—and loaded up a donkey and began the journey to Mount Moriah.

Winston: *(Speaks to Cletus.)* Isaac, my son.

Cletus: *(Looks around and chews on fingernails. Doesn't respond to Winston.)*

Winston: *(Leans toward Cletus.)* Oh, Isaac.

Cletus: *(Looks up and down. Doesn't respond.)*

Winston: *(Jumps up and down.)* Isaaaaaaaac!

Cletus: *(Looks at Winston and then speaks to an audience member.)* Hey, you look like an Isaac. I think he's talkin' to you! And he looks mad!

Winston: *(Taps Cletus' shoulder.)* I'm talking to you, Cletus!

Cletus: *(Shakes head.)* Then why didn't you say my name?

Winston: *(Very frustrated.)* Because you're playing the part of Isaac! My son. My only son!

Cletus: *(Bends over and laughs.)* Hahahahahahahahaha! That's right. Sorry. Go again.

Winston: Isaac, my son—my only son.

Cletus: *(As if reading a script for the first time, almost robotic.)* Yes, Abraham, my father—my one and only father?

Winston: Load up the donkey, and let's go to Mount Moriah to make a special sacrifice.

Cletus: *(Nods head.)* Okey-donkey! *(Walks toward table with Winston.)*

Narrator: *(Looks disapprovingly at Cletus and then clears throat.)* Abraham and Isaac began to gather wood to make an offering. *(Winston and Cletus pretend to gather wood.)*

Abraham Sacrifices Cletus

Winston: *(Wipes sweat from brow.)* Wow. What a journey this has been!

Cletus: *(Looks confused.)* We just took about four steps from over there *(motions to where they were)* to over here *(motions toward table)*. If you're that wore out, you need to see a doctor.

Winston: *(Raises hands in air.)* We're acting! Respect the script!

Cletus: *(Nods head.)* Oh yeah. I forgot! *(Starts panting as if just run a marathon. Grabs spray bottle and sprays face and underarms.)* Look at how much I'm sweatin'! *(Sprays Winston.)* You're sweatin' too, Daddy! *(Sprays some of the audience.)* They're sweatin' too. Wow! Oh, wow! Seriously. I'm so tired and hot and…

Narrator: *(Speaks sternly to Cletus.)* Okay, that's enough!

Cletus: *(Hangs head.)* Sorry.

Winston: *(Motions to Cletus.)* Son, help me pile up this wood to make an altar for our sacrifice.

Cletus: *(Whispers to Winston.)* I don't see no wood.

Winston: *(Motions as if picking up a pile of wood.)* The wood we just picked up! Pretend like we gathered wood.

Cletus: *(Claps hands.)* Oh! I love to pretend. Sometimes I pretend like I'm a superhero. *(Pretends to fly like Superman.)* Sometimes I like to pretend like I'm a race car driver. *(Pretends to steer a race car.)* Sometimes I pretend…

Narrator: *(Jumps up and down and says in a loud voice.)* Just pretend like you're piling up wood for an altar on that table! *(Points to table.)*

Cletus: Sheesh! Okay! *(Pretends to stack wood on table.)*

Narrator: *(Takes another deep breath.)* Once Abraham and Isaac finished preparing the altar, it was time for the sacrifice. The boy, Isaac, was confused and asked what was going to be sacrificed.

Cletus: *(Asks the Narrator.)* Hey, what're we supposed to sacrifice?

Narrator: *(Nods head.)* That's what you're supposed to ask.

Cletus: *(Raises both hands.)* I just did.

Narrator: *(Shakes head.)* No, you're supposed to ask your father, Abraham.

Cletus: Oh. Sorry. *(Taps Winston's shoulder.)* Hey, what're we supposed to sacrifice?

Winston: *(Makes praying hands and looks up.)* God will provide a sacrifice.

Cletus: *(Nods head enthusiastically.)* Ohh…cool. Like something's gonna come flyin' down from heaven to sacrifice. Or God's gonna send a secret agent to bring it? Or is God gonna send it express mail?

Narrator and Winston: *(Loudly)* That's enough!

Cletus: *(Jumps and then hangs head.)* Sorry! I'm just curious!

Narrator: *(Takes a deep breath.)* Abraham—with a sad and heavy heart—asked Isaac to lie down on the altar.

Winston: *(Overly dramatic)* Lie down on the altar, my only son.

Cletus: *(Shrugs shoulders.)* Well, that's weird. But I am kinda tired. *(Lies down on the table.)* Sure is a lot more snuggly than it looks. *(Yawns and begins lightly snoring.)*

Narrator: With Abraham's son—his only son—lying on the altar, Abraham prepared to slay (or kill) his son.

Winston: *(Approaches the altar with hands raised.)*

Cletus: *(Begins to wake up.)* Wait now just a durn minute. Did I hear someone say the word *slay*, as in *kill*—and not as in Christmas *sleigh* bells?

Winston: *(Makes praying hands.)* Please, my son—my only son—lie down on the altar. God has provided.

Cletus: *(Shakes head.)* I didn't know that "provided" actually meant "I'm gonna kill you, Cletus!"

Narrator: *(Notices that things might be getting out of hand.)* However, before Abraham could slay his son, an angel of the Lord called to him: "Abraham! Abraham!"

Cletus: *(Taps Winston's shoulder.)* Better get that. Sounds like it's for you.

Winston: *(Looks up.)* Here I am!

Narrator: The angel said to Abraham, "Don't lay a hand on the boy! Do not hurt him in any way, for now I know that you truly fear God. You have not withheld from me even your son, your only son." Then Abraham looked and saw a ram in a thicket.

Cletus: *(Tilts head as if trying to understand.)* A thicket? I can't afford another parking thicket! See you boys later! *(Waves to Winston and the Narrator and then exits.)*

Abraham Sacrifices Cletus

Narrator: *(Tries not to miss a beat.)* Abraham went to the ram and used it as a burnt offering instead of his son. And from then on, Abraham called that place "the Lord will provide." Goodbye, Abraham. *(Waves to Winston as he exits.)* The end.

(Turns to audience.) That concludes this episode of Biblical Theater World. See you next time! *(Waves to audience and then exits.)*

Use these discussion points with your group following the skit.

1. Describe the most difficult decision you've ever made and what made it so hard. Following God can be difficult too. Describe something God tells us to do that isn't very popular with the rest of the world. Explain how we know what God wants us to do. Describe a time following God was difficult for you and why.

2. Tell about a time friends or others made fun of you because of your faith—if ever. Explain what you think the difference is between the happiness we get from obeying God and the "price" we pay to obey him. The walk from where Abraham lived to the place where he was supposed to make his sacrifice took three days. If you were in his position, do you think you would've changed your mind during that long walk? Why or why not?

3. Talk about where you go when you have to make hard decisions. Why do you think that place helps you think?

4. Abraham changed the name of the place where he was going to sacrifice his son. The name, in Abraham's language, meant "the Lord will provide." Explain whether you think God knows everything, even before it happens. Explain whether you think we get to make up our lives as we go. Talk about how involved you think God is in your life and why.

Abraham Sacrifices Cletus

Red Man Stew

Purpose: Jacob steals Esau's birthright, narrated by a waiter serving up the famous "Red Man Stew." This skit shows jealousy and greed in early biblical sibling rivalry.

Passage: Genesis 25:19-34

People: Jacob, Esau, Narrator

Props:
- plastic spoons (1 per person)
- 3 copies of the skit

Prep: You can be the Narrator (or ask another volunteer to). Choose two people to play the roles of Jacob and Esau. Give each actor a copy of the skit.

Give a plastic spoon to each audience member.

Note to Director: Prior to the skit, tell the kids, "Every time you hear the word *soup*, raise your spoons in the air and say 'Yu-u-m-m-my.' Stretch out the word *yummy* and make it fun!"

Narrator: *(Upbeat, keeps the skit moving.)* Hello, and welcome to our cafe! I'll be your waiter for the day. Would you like to try our special? It's called Red Man Stew! *(Speaks to audience.)* What's that? You've never heard of Red Man Stew? Why, it's our specialty! The recipe is handed down from a man named Jacob. The stew is named after Jacob's brother, Esau. When Esau was born, he was very red and covered with thick hair like fur *(motions to face and arms)*. Jacob made some stew, and Esau loved that stew so much that we named it "Red Man Stew." In fact, Esau, loved the stew so *very* much that he sold his birthright to Jacob for a bowl of it!

(Tilts head as if listening to audience.) What's that? You've never heard of a birthright? Well, back in those days, the son who was born first in the family got some pretty special stuff—stuff that the other kids in the family didn't get, like more money and more land. Sometimes this made the younger kids in the family jealous, so they'd fight about it. No fight over a birthright is more famous than the one that happened between Jacob and Esau, which is why no food is more famous than Red Man Stew!

(Tilts head again and keeps speaking to audience.) What's that? You've never heard of anything as ridiculous as a fight that happens over a bowl of *soup*?

Audience: *(Holds spoons in air.)* Yummy!

Narrator: Well, maybe it'd help if you heard about it from the brothers *(gestures with both hands)*, Jacob and Esau.

Jacob: *(Enters from one side of stage.)* I have a twin brother, but we're nothing alike. For one thing, he smells.

Esau: *(Enters from opposite side of stage.)* I like to hunt and be outdoors. You know—man stuff. *(Sniffs armpit and then looks back to audience.)* Okay, maybe I do smell a little...a little like *awesome*!

Jacob: *(Rolls eyes.)* Esau isn't just smelly. He's also hairy! Which must help him out a lot when he's hunting, because from a distance, he looks like an animal! I could probably hunt just as well as he does, but I'm not a big, hairy beast. I like it indoors—and I love to cook.

Esau: *(Places hands on hips.)* Well, I'd rather be a stinky, hairy hunter than a hairless little mama's boy! *(Mockingly)* Look at me, I like to make *soup*! *(Pretends to stir soup in a prissy manner.)*

Audience: *(Holds spoons in air.)* Yummy!

Jacob: *(Places hands on hips as well.)* Oh yeah? Go ahead and make fun if you want, but you and I both know how much you love my *soup*!

Audience: *(Holds spoons in air.)* Yummy!

Esau: *(Rolls eyes and crosses arms.)* Jacob really does make good *soup*.

Audience: *(Holds spoons in air.)* Yummy!

Esau: *I* usually eat so much of it that my stomach looks like this. *(Pooches out stomach to look big and round.)*

Jacob: I guess you could say it's priceless, right, Esau? *(Winks at audience and then speaks to audience.)* You see, a few days ago, Esau came in all smelly and sweaty after hunting, and I'd just finished making my special *soup*.

Audience: *(Holds spoons in air.)* Yummy!

Jacob: *(Tilts head toward Esau.)* Esau was hungry.

Esau: *(Places both hands on stomach.)* I was so hungry that I would've put my whole head in that pot if it hadn't been so hot!

Jacob: *(Nods head.)* Oh, I could tell. So I decided this might be a good time to offer Esau a trade I'd been thinking about.

Esau: Yeah, because this one here *(nods head toward Jacob)* not only knows how to stir up stew but can stir up a whole pot of trouble, too. And he uses some pretty strong ingredients, like jealousy! *(Turns head quickly toward Jacob and glares at him.)*

Jacob: *(Looks at Esau.)* Well, for such a manly hunter, you were pretty easy prey.

Esau: *(Looks at audience.)* I've never been so hungry! *(Turns to Jacob.)* Not that you'd know what it's like to work up such an appetite!

Jacob: *(Looks at Esau.)* That was a pretty expensive dinner, wasn't it, bro?

Esau: *(Turns to Jacob and gets irritated.)* I'll say it was! What kind of brother asks for a birthright in exchange for a bowl of *soup*?

Audience: *(Holds spoons in air.)* Yummy!

Jacob: *(Turns to Esau, gets in his face, and starts to yell.)* Oh, probably no worse than a brother who's willing to give up his inheritance for a sloppy slurp of food!

Narrator: *(Steps between the brothers to break them up.)* Well, that'll do, fellas. I think they get the point. *(Turns to audience.)* Now, as a waiter, I rely on tips to make a living. But today I'll leave you with a tip instead. Go ahead and try the *soup*.

Audience: *(Holds spoons in air.)* Yummy!

Narrator: But never pay more than it's worth!

Red Man Stew

Use these discussion points with your group following the skit.

1. Describe an imaginary person who's the exact opposite of you in every possible way, and give that person a name. Explain what you think it would be like to grow up with that person. Tell about a time in real life you had to make friends with someone you had nothing in common with.

2. Esau's choice to sell his birthright seems like a foolish one. But we've all made foolish choices. Why do we sometimes make bad choices, even when we know it's a bad idea?

3. Think about the typical family portrait that hangs on a wall in someone's home. Explain whether you think those kinds of family portraits are accurate—and why or why not. Explain whether you think we should strive for the "happy portrait" or just be real in our families.

4. Esau might not have been the sharpest knife in the drawer, but he seemed to be a good son. He didn't run off after Jacob left; he stayed and took care of his family. And yet he gave up the birthright for a bowl of stew. How do you think we can focus on the big picture and not get distracted by the little things in front of us in the moment?

5. Jacob's jealousy may have caused the problem, but it was his pride that kept him from fixing the problem. Explain how you think pride can get in the way of our relationships with our families. How can it get in the way of our relationships with God?

Bad Boys, Bad Boys—Whatcha Gonna Do?

Purpose: Joseph's brothers sell him into slavery. Kids will hear Joseph's brothers confess their bad choices. They'll learn how we hurt others when we let hatred rule our hearts.

Passage: Genesis 37:5-36

People: Brothers 1 and 2, Judah, Reuben, Cop

Props:
- 4 chairs
- colorful robe
- 5 copies of the skit

Prep: You can play the Cop (or choose another volunteer to). Choose four others to be the four brothers. Give each actor a copy of the skit.

Set the chairs side by side, facing the audience. Have Brother 1 sit far left, followed by Brother 2, Judah, and then Reuben. Place the colorful robe out of sight but within easy reach.

Note to Director: Prior to the skit, tell the audience they'll respond to questions the Cop asks them—either "yes" or "no."

Cop: *(Stands in front of the four brothers and faces audience.)* Hello, good citizens. My name is Officer Kris P. Kreemer. I appreciate that you're here today so you can help our fine department decide whether or not to charge these four brothers with criminal mischief. *(Moves to stand behind Brother 1 in far left chair.)* I'll start by introducing the perps. These are the brothers of our victim, Joseph. *(Starts walking behind brothers.)* We received a tip that these men were responsible for selling Joseph as a slave. *(Paces back toward other side.)* We've brought the brothers in for questioning. I'd appreciate your input as we find out the facts of the case.

(Stands behind Brother 1, puts hands on his shoulders, and speaks to him.) Now from what I understand, you were in a town called Dothan, tending some sheep. Is that correct?

Brother 1: *(Nods head to audience.)* Yes, that's right.

Cop: You saw your brother Joseph heading toward you from a distance?

Brother 1: Yes. *(Comments quietly but so audience can hear.)* Little brat.

Cop: *(Leans down to Brother 1's face.)* What's that?

Brother 1: *(Grumbles)* Nothing. Yes, we saw Joseph coming.

Cop: *(Moves behind Brother 2.)* Were you happy to see him?

Brother 2: *(Shakes head and speaks to audience.)* Not really, no. *(Brother 1 and Judah elbow him.)*

Cop: So what'd you say to your brothers?

Brother 2: *(Looks down at lap.)* Here comes that doofus. *(Looks up, startled, catches self.)* I mean, dreamer! Here comes that dreamer!

Cop: What do you mean by "dreamer"?

Brother 2: Aw, he was always having dreams about how one day he would rule over us. It was *so* annoying.

Cop: *(Moves behind Judah, puts hands on his shoulders, and speaks to him.)* Then what did your brothers say, Judah? You're Judah, right?

Judah: *(Nods head.)* My brothers said, "Let's *(coughs and puts fisted hand in front of mouth while saying the word "kill," making sure audience hears the word)* kill him."

Cop: *(Asks audience.)* Did you catch that, good citizens? What'd he say they wanted to do to Joseph? Hug him? *(Shakes head and encourages audience to shout.)*

Audience: No!

Cop: *(Speaks to audience)* That's what I thought! The brothers wanted to kill Joseph. *(Moves behind Reuben.)* Now, Reuben! That's your name, right? *(Reuben nods head.)* You didn't like the sound of that, did you?

Reuban: *(Shakes head and speaks to audience.)* No, I didn't.

Cop: So you didn't want to kill Joseph, but you offered another suggestion. What was it?

Reuban: *(Hangs head, ashamed.)* Throw him into an empty water tank. It's like a well.

Cop: *(Asks audience.)* Does that sound like a good way to treat a brother? *(Shakes head and encourages audience to shout.)*

Audience: No!

Cop: I don't think so either. *(To Reuben)* What did you plan to do after you threw Joseph into the well?

Reuban: *(Glances at brothers.)* Rescue Joseph and take him back to our dad. But when I went back to save him, he was gone. *(Brothers all fold their arms and glare at Reuben.)*

Cop: *(Moves in front of Reuben and talks to audience.)* So it sounds like Reuben here was trying to do the right thing. Do you think I should arrest him? *(Shakes head and encourages audience to shout.)*

Audience: No!

Cop: *(Turns and talks to Reuben face to face.)* Reuben, you made a good choice. You did the right thing. You're free to go.

Reuban: *(Gets up and goes to sit down in audience. Audience claps for Reuben.)*

Cop: *(Grabs the robe from the side of the stage and stands in front of the remaining brothers. Dangles the robe in front of their faces.)* So tell me about this. *(All the brothers shrug, looking at each other. Cop moves to stand behind Judah.)*

Judah: It was hot! We took Joseph's robe off. No big deal. *(Looks at brothers.)*

Cop: *(Holds up robe.)* This robe looks pretty fancy. From what I understand, Joseph was the only one in the family who got one.

(Asks audience) Sounds to me like these guys might've been a little jealous! What do you think? *(Nods and encourages audience to shout.)*

Audience: Yes!

Bad Boys, Bad Boys—Whatcha Gonna Do?

Cop: *(Stands behind Brother 1.)* So you help Joseph out of his robe. Then what?

Brother 1: We put him in the shade. *(Looks at brothers and winks.)*

Cop: In the shade, you say? *(Stands behind Brother 2.)* And where was this shady spot located?

Brother 2: *(Throws hands up, tired of the questioning.)* In the well! The shade was in the well! *(Other brothers elbow him.)* But we got him out later! *(Glares at brothers.)*

Cop: Yes, you did! This is the part I know! *(Speaks to audience.)* My sources tell me that the brothers took Joseph out of the well and sold him as a slave for 20 pieces of silver! Does that sound like a good way to treat your brother? *(Shakes head and encourages audience to shout.)*

Audience: No!

Cop: *(Grabs robe and holds it up to audience. Stands in front of brothers and points to a spot on the robe.)* And this is blood. It was examined and found to be the blood of a goat. *(Turns to face brothers and holds robe out to them.)* But that's not what you wanted your dad to think when you took it back to your house, was it? *(Brothers all look down, ashamed.)*

(Turns back around to face audience.) Your dad's too upset to be here today. He's crushed. He believes his son Joseph is dead because that's what you *(points behind at brothers)* told him. Your dad believes an animal has killed Joseph. A lie. So given the way these brothers treated Joseph, the way they planned to kill him, and the way they lied to their father, should I arrest them? *(Nods head and encourages audience to shout.)*

Audience: Yes!

Cop: All right then. *(Turns to side of stage, cups hands around mouth, and shouts.)* Deputy Decaf, let's book 'em!

Use these discussion points with your group following the skit.

1. Joseph had nighttime dreams that the universe revolved around him and that someday his brothers would bow down before him. Then he made the mistake of actually *telling* his brothers his dreams. Explain whether you can understand why his brothers sold him.

2. Explain whether you think God still uses dreams to speak to us.

3. The first six words of this passage in the Bible are "One night Joseph had a dream." Explain what your dreams are for the future. Tell about the kinds of things you'd like to have happen in your life.

4. Tell about a time you shared a dream with someone and that person laughed at it or made fun of you. Explain why you think people sometimes laugh at others' dreams.

5. An author named Richard Bach once wrote, "You're never given a dream without also being given the power to make it true." Explain whether you agree or disagree with this statement and why. Explain whether you think any dream can come true without the person having to work for it.

6. Joseph's dreams came true. He became the leader of a nation, and his brothers bowed down to him. But he couldn't have been the leader of a nation by being the spoiled little brat he was at the beginning of the passage. He had to undergo massive hardships that made him into a different person. Describe something you've had to leave behind in your life to become a new person.

Bad Boys, Bad Boys—Whatcha Gonna Do?

Fuhgeddaboudit

Percolator

Purpose: Joseph forgives his brothers, as witnessed "live" on Orpah's TV show.

Passage: Genesis 42:1–45:28

People: Orpah, Simeon, Joseph, Sign Holder/Announcer

Props:
- poster board
- marker
- 3 chairs
- 4 copies of the skit

Prep: Ask someone to play the role of Orpah, an over-the-top daytime television host. Choose two people to be the brothers Simeon and Joseph. Have another person be the Sign Holder/Announcer. Give each person a copy of the skit.

Write "Applause!" on one side of a sheet of poster board and "Gasp!" on the other side.

Set the stage for a daytime talk show—two chairs facing out and angled in toward each other (for the guests) and the other chair close by (for the host).

Note to Director: Prior to the skit, practice the audience responses. Alternately hold up the "Applause" sign and then the "Gasp!" sign. Encourage kids to be enthusiastic in their responses.

Fuhgeddaboudit

Announcer: *(From offstage)* And now for our amazingly talented—and not at all overly dramatic—host you love to love who loves to love…Orpah, ladies and gentlemen!

(SIGN HOLDER RUNS ACROSS STAGE WITH "APPLAUSE" SIGN.)

Orpah: *(Enters, smiling and waving to guests, and sits in "host" chair.)* Thank you, everyone, and welcome to Egypt's number-one talk show—my show! Today's topic is forgiveness, and we have an amazing show for you. One of our guests was thrown in prison, but he doesn't really know why. Let's get to the bottom of it! Simeon! Welcome to the show!

(SIGN HOLDER RUNS ACROSS STAGE WITH "APPLAUSE" SIGN.)

Simeon: *(Enters and sits on a chair near Orpah.)* Hello, Orpah. Thank you for having me on your show.

Orpah: Simeon, why don't you tell our audience *(motions with both hands toward audience)* a little bit about yourself? What brought you to us here in Egypt?

Simeon: *(Looks at audience.)* Uh, my name is Simeon. I'm one of 12 brothers.

Orpah: *(Sits up straight and looks impressed.)* That's a lot of brothers!

Simeon: Well, 11 brothers now. One of them is gone. But that was a long, long time ago. My brothers and I are here because there's been a terrible famine—nothing to eat! *(Places hands on stomach.)*

Orpah: *(Spreads arms wide.)* Here in Egypt we have plenty of food—thanks to our great governor.

(SIGN HOLDER RUNS ACROSS STAGE WITH "APPLAUSE" SIGN.)

Simeon: *(Nods head.)* That's what we heard. So our father sent us here to get food. We did get a chance to meet your great governor. Unfortunately *(shrugs shoulders)*, he didn't believe we were here for food. He thought we were spies.

Orpah: So is that how you became a prisoner here?

Simeon: Well, like I said, the governor didn't believe that we were just looking for food. *(Holds palms up.)* We told him we were 10 brothers who came to buy food for our families back home in Canaan and that our dad and little brother, Benjamin, were still back home waiting for us. *(Rubs forehead in frustration.)* He said that one of us had to stay here in prison until the other brothers went all the way back to Canaan and brought back Benjamin to prove our story!

Orpah: *(Nods head.)* Well, Simeon…it was brave for you to stay here and become a prisoner to help save your other brothers.

Simeon: *(Hangs head.)* Well, I haven't always been a brave brother.

Orpah: Hmmm, I see. *(Tilts head.)* So did your brothers go to Canaan and come back?

Simeon: *(Nods head.)* Yes, my brothers came back for me and brought Benji with them. My dad almost didn't let them bring Benji. Dad had already lost one of his sons a long time ago—my little brother Joseph. But the governor was clear that he wanted to see Benji.

Orpah: *(Leans toward Simeon while asking questions.)* When your brothers came back to Egypt, what happened then? Did the governor believe you were here for food?

Simeon: He did! He believed our story, and he even invited us all over to a big feast at his house. The food was great, but…*(Sighs deeply.)* It was weird. We were sitting there eating, and we noticed that we were all sitting in order from oldest to youngest around this big table. I mean, that's strange, right? The governor knew we were brothers, but how could he possibly know what order we were born in?

Orpah: Strange. *(Shakes head.)* So what happened next?

Simeon: We were on our way home with all the food we'd just bought when all these Egyptian guards came running after us. *(Places hands on chest, as if surprised.)* They said we'd stolen the governor's favorite silver cup.

Orpah: And that's why you're all being held as prisoners in Egypt?

Simeon: *(Nods head.)* Yeah, I guess so.

Orpah: Now, Simeon, I have a surprise guest backstage who wants to speak to you. *(To audience)* Why don't we bring out our special surprise guest to help us shed a little light on this problem? Whaddaya think, audience? Should we bring him out?

(SIGN HOLDER RUNS ACROSS STAGE WITH "APPLAUSE" SIGN.)

Orpah: All right then. Ladies and gentlemen, please welcome our surprise guest, the governor of Egypt! *(Stands and leads everyone in applause.)*

(SIGN HOLDER RUNS ACROSS STAGE WITH "APPLAUSE" SIGN.)

Joseph: *(Enters, smiling and waving, and then sits on the other chair.)* Hello, Orpah. Thanks for having me on your show.

Orpah: *(Places hand to chest.)* Governor, let me first say what an honor it is to have you here. Thanks for coming.

Joseph: *(Bows slightly in a "royal" way.)* Thank you, Orpah. I wish I could've been here under different circumstances. Ya see, I came here because one of these brothers *(motions to Simeon)* stole my favorite silver cup, and I'm here to tell you that we've figured out which one of these brothers took it. We found my favorite silver cup in…*(stands and points to the back of the audience as though looking at Benjamin)* Benjamin's backpack! And now Benjamin will be a prisoner in Egypt for the rest of his life!

(SIGN HOLDER RUNS ACROSS STAGE WITH "GASP!" SIGN.)

Simeon: *(Suddenly stands before Joseph.)* Governor! Please! There must be some mistake! *(Falls to knees in front of Joseph.)* Please, take me instead. Keep me as your prisoner, and don't take Benji.

Joseph: You'd take your brother's place in prison?

Simeon: *(Bows head.)* Yes, I would.

Orpah: *(Looks at Joseph.)* Governor…I think it's time to reveal to our audience who you really are.

Joseph: *(Helps Simeon up.)* Simeon…*(to audience)* all my brothers…I know you don't recognize me. It's been such a long time…*(Takes a deep breath.)* I'm your brother, Joseph!

Simeon: *(In shock, moves away—a little afraid.)* It can't be!

Joseph: *(Throws arm around Simeon.)* Get over here, man! Don't be afraid. I'm not going to hurt you! I'm so glad to see all of you! Now we can all be one big, happy family again!

Simeon: *(Confused and still a little timid.)* But aren't you mad at us for…ya know…selling you to be a slave?

Joseph: Nah. *(Holds Simeon out with both hands at arms' length.)* Forgive and fuhgeddaboudit! *(Turns Simeon toward audience.)* God has taken my life and blessed it. See? Now I'm governor of Egypt and get to help save people's lives during this great famine. And now I get to save yours, too. All of you, my brothers, and Father—you'll all come live with me and enjoy the blessing God has given me!

(SIGN HOLDER RUNS ACROSS STAGE WITH "APPLAUSE" SIGN.)

Orpah: (*Wipes tears from eyes and joins Joseph and Simeon for a group hug.*) I just love bringing families together! (*Waves to audience.*) Thanks for joining us on the show! See you tomorrow! (*Orpah, Joseph, and Simeon exit.*)

(*SIGN HOLDER RUNS TO CENTER STAGE WITH "APPLAUSE" SIGN, BENDS OVER AT WAIST—BREATHING DEEPLY AS IF TRYING TO RECOVER FROM SO MUCH EXERCISE—AND THEN WAVES AND EXITS.*)

sticky Talk

Use these discussion points with your group following the skit.

1. This skit is a lot like a talk show we'd see on TV today. Describe your reaction to the drama that was in Joseph's life.

2. Tell about the most annoying thing your sibling or another family member does. What's the most annoying thing you've ever done to a family member? Why do you think family members do those annoying things to each other when they wouldn't treat common strangers that way?

3. What sort of advice would you give to your children if they couldn't get along? What kind of advice do you think God gives us—his children—about getting along?

4. Joseph's brothers had done terrible things to him, but he found the strength to forgive them anyway. This strength was part of his character, and it helped him become a leader of a nation, and to help rule that nation well and wisely. Tell about a time you forgave someone. How did that affect your relationship with that person? Why is it important to forgive others?

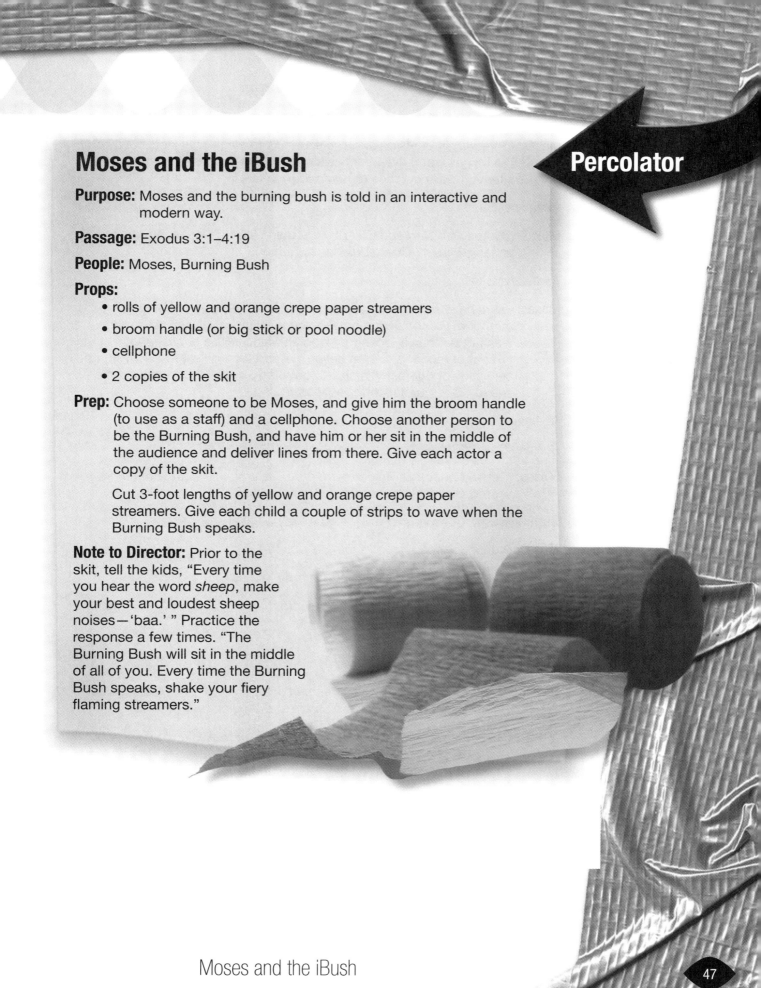

Moses and the iBush

Purpose: Moses and the burning bush is told in an interactive and modern way.

Passage: Exodus 3:1–4:19

People: Moses, Burning Bush

Props:
- rolls of yellow and orange crepe paper streamers
- broom handle (or big stick or pool noodle)
- cellphone
- 2 copies of the skit

Prep: Choose someone to be Moses, and give him the broom handle (to use as a staff) and a cellphone. Choose another person to be the Burning Bush, and have him or her sit in the middle of the audience and deliver lines from there. Give each actor a copy of the skit.

Cut 3-foot lengths of yellow and orange crepe paper streamers. Give each child a couple of strips to wave when the Burning Bush speaks.

Note to Director: Prior to the skit, tell the kids, "Every time you hear the word *sheep*, make your best and loudest sheep noises—'baa.' " Practice the response a few times. "The Burning Bush will sit in the middle of all of you. Every time the Burning Bush speaks, shake your fiery flaming streamers."

Moses and the iBush

Moses: *(Enters from one side of stage and talks to audience.)* Hey, everybody! I'm Moses…and I've been walking all over this mountain looking for my *sheep!* *(Cues audience to respond.)*

Audience: Baa!

Moses: *(Jumps as if startled.)* Oh! There you are! Nice little sheepy, sheepy, sheepy, *sheep!* *(Cues audience to respond.)*

Audience: Baa!

Moses: I sure have some great adventures to tell. God loves getting my attention. *(Bends over a bit and sounds winded.)* Whew, this mountain was farther than it looked by Google Maps. *(Pulls out cellphone.)* I bet I'm out of range. *(Looks at cellphone and then puts it to ear.)* Yep, no service. Not one bar. It's nice to get off by myself—just me and the *sheep*. *(Cues audience to respond.)*

Audience: Baa!

Burning Bush: *(Cues kids to wave streamers.)* Moses!

Moses: *(Doesn't notice waving streamers. Turns around a couple of times, scared, and looks for source of voice.)* What?!

Burning Bush: *(Cues kids to wave streamers.)* Moses!

Moses: *(Keeps looking and talks into cellphone.)* Yes?

Burning Bush: *(Cues kids to wave streamers.)* Moses!

Moses: *(Shakes cellphone and then yells into it.)* Hello? Can you hear me now?

Burning Bush: *(Cues kids to wave streamers.)* Moses, look over here.

Moses: *(Finally notices waving streamers.)* Whoa! Who are you?

Burning Bush: *(Cues kids to wave streamers.)* I am the God of your ancestors. Take off your shoes. You are standing on holy ground.

Moses: Oh, yeah! Okay! *(Hops from foot to foot and makes a big display of taking off one shoe and then the other. Takes a deep breath and then shakes phone again.)* You get service up here, God?

Burning Bush: *(Cues kids to wave streamers.)* I get service everywhere. I have a job for you.

Moses: But I have a job. I'm in the family business. See? *(Gestures to audience.)* Sheep! *(Cues audience to respond.)*

Audience: Baa!

Burning Bush: *(Cues kids to wave streamers.)* I need you to go back to Egypt and bring my people—the Israelites—home.

Moses: *(Taps phone.)* I think we have a bad connection. It sounded like you said to go back to Egypt. *(Shouts into phone.)* Can you still hear me now?

Burning Bush: *(Cues kids to wave streamers.)* Moses, I know your past. I know your problems. I know everything, and I'm choosing you to go.

Moses: *(Tilts head.)* Are you sure?

Burning Bush: *(Shouts and cues kids to wave streamers.)* I am!

Moses: *(Looks scared.)* The people of Egypt know my faults too. What if they won't listen to me? I can't go. I have a bunch of stuff I need to do… remember? *(Gestures to audience.)* Sheep! *(Cues audience to respond.)*

Audience: Baa!

Burning Bush: *(Cues kids to wave streamers.)* I'll be with you. You can message me any time.

Moses: *(Shakes head.)* They'll never listen to me.

Burning Bush: *(Cues kids to wave streamers.)* Tell them the God of their ancestors Abraham, Isaac, and Jacob sent you.

Moses: *(Shakes head again.)* Suppose I go and I tell them the God of their ancestors sent me and they ask me, "What's his name?" What do I tell them? Is there an app for that? *(Looks at phone.)*

Burning Bush: *(Cues kids to wave streamers.)* I am.

Moses: *(Looks puzzled.)* Huh? IM? Instant Message?

Burning Bush: *(Cues kids to wave streamers.)* Not IM. *(Takes a deep breath.)* I AM! Tell them "I AM sent me to you."

Moses: *(Shakes phone.)* Reception must've gotten bad again. *(Puts phone to ear and shouts.)* Can you hear me now? What?

Burning Bush: *(Cues kids to wave streamers.)* Moses, trust me. I've got you covered. Now go! Your father-in-law is waiting for you to bring back his *sheep. (Cues audience to respond.)*

Audience: Baa!

Burning Bush: *(Cues kids to wave streamers.)* You have a big journey ahead of you, Moses.

Moses: *(Says to the audience as exits.)* I gotta get a different data plan...

Moses and the iBush

sticky Talk

Use these discussion points with your group following the skit.

1. Explain whether you think God has trouble getting our attention. Think about someone who's texting while walking and proceeds to walk into a wall. Explain whether you think that's like our relationship with God.

2. God (through the bush) tells Moses to take off his shoes because he's on sacred ground. Explain what you think *sacred* means. What do you think makes something sacred? Describe the most sacred room in our church. Describe something you own that's sacred to you—even if it isn't to someone else. Explain how you think special objects or locations like our sacred places open us up to God's Word.

3. Tell why you think God didn't tell Moses his name.

4. Moses held a position of great authority before he got demoted to shepherd. Explain whether you'd rather be in charge of the church-building committee or work with a flock of sheep and why. Why do you suppose one of the most famous references to God is "The Lord is my Shepherd"?

5. Moses tried to get out of the job God gave him several times. He told God he couldn't speak well; he told God they wouldn't listen; he told God he didn't want to go by himself; he told God he wouldn't know what words to use. God answered all of Moses' concerns—mostly by saying, "I'm with you." Think about the hardest part of your life right now. Now imagine God saying, "I'm with you." Imagine God saying it over and over. What do you think it takes for us to believe God really is with us?

Pharaoh's Freeze Dance

Instant

Purpose: The 10 plagues are told in a rhyme with motions. Kids will learn about Pharaoh's stubbornness and God's faithfulness to the Israelites.

Passage: Exodus 7:14–11:10

People: Narrator, Assistant

Props:
- CD (upbeat, instrumental children's ministry music)
- CD player
- 2 copies of the skit

Prep: You can be the Narrator (or ask another volunteer to). Choose someone to be the Assistant, and give him or her a copy of the skit. After the Narrator announces each plague, the Assistant plays music and cues the kids for each move. The Assistant should also have access to the lights. When the music stops, the kids stop moving.

Note to Director: Before the skit, practice these moves (encourage kids to freestyle and use their imaginations, too):

1. Water to blood—pretend to step in blood and be grossed out by it.
2. Frogs—hop around like frogs.
3. Gnats—slap arms and face as if being attacked by gnats.
4. Flies—swat in the air at flies.
5. Dead Animals—hold nose and shout "Ew!"
6./7. Boils and Hail—put hands on head and arms, run around, and shout "Ow!"
8. Locusts—drop to the floor and curl up in a ball.
9. Darkness—turn off lights and everyone scream.
10. Firstborn Death—pretend to hold a baby and cry.

Narrator: The Lord said to Moses, "Pharaoh's heart is hard like steel.

Lead him down to the river, 'cause it's 'bout to get real."

So Moses did as he was told

And waved with his wand.

The water all turned to blood

And grossed out the pond!

(ASSISTANT PLAYS CD. KIDS PRETEND TO STEP IN BLOOD AND BE GROSSED OUT BY IT. AFTER A FEW SECONDS, ASSISTANT PAUSES CD.)

Narrator: Seven days later, Pharaoh's mind was still not changed.

Moses tried to warn him, "Frogs are coming! What a pain!"

Pharaoh blew him off, and so over all the ground

Came a slimy bunch of frogs, hipping-hopping all around!

(ASSISTANT PLAYS CD. KIDS HOP AROUND LIKE FROGS. AFTER A FEW SECONDS, ASSISTANT PAUSES CD.)

Narrator: Pharaoh said, "Hey, Moses, would you pray these frogs away?"

Moses did it and they croaked, but a yucky smell stayed.

Pharaoh's heart went hard again, just as God had predicted.

So the third plague came—it was with *gnats* that God afflicted!

(ASSISTANT PLAYS CD. KIDS SLAP ARMS AND FACE AS IF BEING ATTACKED BY GNATS. AFTER A FEW SECONDS, ASSISTANT PAUSES CD.)

Narrator: Moses tried and tried, but Pharaoh wouldn't listen.

Three plagues already came, but the point he still was missin'.

So the Lord sent his people off into the land of Goshen;

Then Egypt swarmed with flies like a buzzing black ocean!

(ASSISTANT PLAYS CD. KIDS SWAT IN THE AIR AT FLIES. AFTER A FEW SECONDS, ASSISTANT PAUSES CD.)

Narrator: With another prayer from Moses, the flies went away.

So Pharaoh took a chill pill,

But the peace, it wouldn't stay.

Plague number five was bad for animals in Egypt.

They all got sick and died

And the whole place smelled like vomit! (Nothing rhymes with Egypt!)

(ASSISTANT PLAYS CD. KIDS HOLD NOSES AND SHOUT "EW!" AFTER A FEW SECONDS, ASSISTANT PAUSES CD.)

Narrator: As if this wasn't bad enough for Pharaoh's epic fail—

The sixth and seventh plagues were coming, and they *hurt*!

God sent boils and hail!

(ASSISTANT PLAYS CD. KIDS PUT HANDS ON HEAD AND ARMS, RUN AROUND, AND SHOUT "OW!" AFTER A FEW SECONDS, ASSISTANT PAUSES CD.)

Narrator: His noggin, bumped and bruised, was still not thinking straight.

Pharaoh broke a third promise, and on came plague number eight!

Locusts everywhere, eating everything in sight!

So numerous and noisy—nobody slept at night!

(ASSISTANT PLAYS CD. KIDS DROP TO FLOOR AND CURL UP IN A BALL. AFTER A FEW SECONDS, ASSISTANT PAUSES CD.)

Narrator: Night. That's what came next.

And all of Egypt went pitch black.

The ninth plague was a doozy—

Not a person could see smack!

(ASSISTANT PLAYS CD AND TURNS OFF LIGHTS. EVERYONE SCREAMS. AFTER A FEW SECONDS, ASSISTANT PAUSES CD AND TURNS LIGHTS BACK ON.)

Pharaoh's Freeze Dance

Narrator: Three days this stayed in Egypt

With the lights completely out.

But the Israelites had sunshine

And were skipping all about!

Ten was really horrible, the saddest one of all.

It affected all the firstborn, some were very, very small.

God did not want to do it—letting all those children die.

The parents of these babies

Would be so, so sad and cry.

(ASSISTANT PLAYS CD. KIDS PRETEND TO HOLD A BABY AND CRY. AFTER A FEW SECONDS, ASSISTANT PAUSES CD.)

Narrator: But with the use of lamb's blood painted on their doors,

Death passed right by the Israelites,

The plagues would be no more.

God delivered them from Pharaoh

And the Israelites were free.

They'd have a great, great memory

Of how God loved them faithfully!

(ASSISTANT PLAYS CD. NARRATOR ENCOURAGES KIDS TO FREESTYLE DANCE AND MOVE. AFTER A FEW SECONDS, ASSISTANT SHUTS OFF CD. NARRATOR LEADS EVERYONE IN TAKING A BOW.)

sticKy Talk

Use these discussion points with your group following the skit.

1. Consider this list of the 10 plagues: blood, frogs, gnats, flies, dead animals, boils, hail, locusts, darkness, and death. Find a few friends to work with, and see if you can come up with modern-day equivalents for each plague.

2. The Bible says Pharaoh's heart was hardened. What do you think it means to have a hard heart? Explain whether you think having a hard heart is a choice. Describe the kinds of things you think can cause someone to have a hard heart.

3. What are some "unbreakable" rules in your family? (Example: No texting at the dinner table.) Think about one of these rules, and talk with your group about the consequences of breaking the rule. Explain why you think this rule and punishment are in place. Tell whether you think it's easy for parents to punish their children and why.

4. There's a Jewish celebration called Passover. (This is what Jesus and his disciples were celebrating when the Last Supper took place.) It's a celebration of the way God cares for his children. How do you think God takes care of us as a church? Describe how God has taken care of you personally.

Pharaoh's Freeze Dance

Moses Takes a Trip

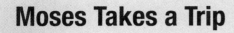

Purpose: The Ten Commandments are told by Moses to an airport Customs Agent.

Passage: Exodus 19:16–20:21

People: Narrator, Moses, Customs Agent

Props:

- table
- suitcase
- 10 random items (such as a stapler, stuffed animal, pillow, and so on)
- 3 copies of the skit

Prep: Set the table center stage.

Select 10 random objects from the room and put them in the suitcase. This is an improvisational skit, so the sillier the items the better!

You can be the Narrator (or ask another volunteer to). Choose two others to be Moses and the Customs Agent. Give Moses the suitcase, and give each actor a copy of the skit.

Note to Director: During the skit, kids will come, one at a time, to choose an item from the suitcase, interact with the Customs Agent, and then proceed through customs and back to their seat. Prompts are noted throughout the script.

Narrator: *(Stands to one side of stage.)* After spending some time with God atop Mount Sinai, Moses realized he needed to get back to his people.

Moses: *(Enters from one side of stage carrying suitcase. Takes a few steps and then looks up.)* All right, God. It's been great spending time with you up on Mount Sinai, but it looks like I have a flight to catch. I'll see you later. *(Walks toward the table.)*

Narrator: When Moses arrived at the airport, a Customs Agent asked Moses to declare what he'd brought back with him from his time with God.

Customs Agent: *(Enters from opposite side and joins Moses center stage by the table.)* Welcome back from Mount Sinai. I hope you had a pleasant trip.

Moses: *(Nods head.)* Why, thank you. I had a marvelous time.

Customs Agent: *(Tilts head.)* What was the nature of your trip to Mount Sinai?

Moses: Business and pleasure, I suppose. I was able to spend some quality time with God, but I also managed to bring back some laws that he gave me *(places suitcase on table)*.

Customs Agent: *(Places hands on suitcase.)* Laws, you say?

Moses: *(Nods head.)* That's right. The Ten Commandments, actually.

Customs Agent: Ten, huh? *(Motions to suitcase.)* Better get those out so I can inspect them.

Moses: *(Opens suitcase.)* All right.

Narrator: And so the Ten Commandments were inspected by the Customs Agent.

Customs Agent: Okay. Let's get this inspection going so you can be on your way, Moses. *(Chooses a child to come up and pick an item from the suitcase. Takes the object and pretends to read something on it.)* You shall have no other gods before God. *(Holds up object.)* Does this look like a god to you? *(Shakes head and cues audience to respond.)*

Audience: No!

Customs Agent: Okay then. *(Hands object to child.)* Go on through. *(Moses guides child offstage to go sit down.)* Ready? *(Waves to another child.)* What's next?

Child 2: *(Steps forward, grabs an object from the suitcase, and hands it to the agent.)*

Customs Agent: *(Pretends to read from object.)* Don't make idols of any kind, and don't worship them. *(Holds up object.)* Anybody want to bow down to this thing? *(Shakes head and cues audience to respond.)*

Audience: No!

Customs Agent: I should say not! *(Hands object to child.)* Go on through. *(Moses guides child offstage.)* Come on! *(Motions to next child.)* Let's see what's next.

Child 3: *(Steps forward, grabs an object from the suitcase, and hands it to the agent.)*

Customs Agent: *(Pretends to read from object.)* Don't misuse God's name. [Name of object] can't talk, can it? *(Shakes head and cues audience to respond.)*

Audience: No!

Customs Agent: Well, then I guess it can't misuse God's name! *(Hands object to child.)* Go on through! *(Moses guides child offstage.)* Next commandment! *(Motions to another child to come up.)*

Child 4: *(Steps forward, grabs an object from the suitcase, and hands it to the agent.)*

Customs Agent: *(Pretends to read from object.)* Remember the Sabbath and keep it holy. *(Talks to object and tickles it.)* You'll promise to remember, won't you? *(Hands object to child; then Moses helps child offstage.)* Next! *(Motions to another child.)*

Child 5: *(Steps forward, grabs an object from the suitcase, and hands it to the agent.)*

Customs Agent: *(Pretends to read from object.)* The fifth commandment is to honor your father and mother. *(Holds up object.)* I'm happy to say this looks nothing like my mother. *(Hands object to child, and Moses guides child offstage.)* Next! *(Motions to another child to come up.)*

Child 6: *(Steps forward, grabs an object from the suitcase, and hands it to the agent.)*

Customs Agent: *(Pretends to read from object.)* Don't murder. *(Drops object on floor and jumps back.)* Aaaah! You just scared me! Get outta here! *(Kicks object to Moses, and child walks through.)* Let's hope the next commandment is nicer! *(Motions to another child.)* Come through, please!

Moses Takes a Trip

Child 7: *(Steps forward, grabs an object from the suitcase, and hands it to the agent.)*

Customs Agent: *(Pretends to read from object.)* Commandment number seven: Don't commit adultery. Hmm. I agree. The last thing you want to be is an adult. Stay a kid as long as you can! *(Hands object to child, and Moses guides child offstage.)* Next! *(Motions to another child.)*

Child 8: *(Steps forward, grabs an object from the suitcase, and hands it to the agent.)*

Customs Agent: *(Pretends to read from object.)* Don't steal. *(Hurriedly hands object back to child.)* Here, take it back—I promise I wasn't going to keep it! *(Moses guides child offstage.)* Next commandment! *(Motions to another child.)*

Child 9: *(Steps forward, grabs an object from the suitcase, and hands it to the agent.)*

Customs Agent: *(Pretends to read from object.)* Don't lie. *(Turns to audience.)* Okay, I admit it! *(Places hands on stomach.)* That was me. I had beans for lunch. I'm so glad we're almost done with this! *(Gives object to child, and Moses guides child offstage.)* Bring 10 on through! *(Motions to another child.)*

Child 10: *(Steps forward, grabs the last object from the suitcase, and hands it to the agent.)*

Customs Agent: *(Pretends to read from object.)* This is the tenth commandment: Don't covet. *(Turns to Moses.)* Help me out with this one, Moses. What does that even mean?

Moses: It means don't want what others have.

Customs Agent: Oh, gotcha. *(Turns to audience.)* That's gonna be a tough one, isn't it? *(Nods head and cues audience to shout.)*

Audience: Yes!

Customs Agent: *(To Moses)* So what is it that you plan on doing with all these commandments?

Moses: Well, I'm going to share them with everyone, of course. *(Spreads arms wide.)* God wants us to know how we should live, and that's what getting to know all these commandments will do.

Customs Agent: *(Gives suitcase to Moses.)* Well, then you and your friends better get going. *(Moses and Customs Agent wave and exit.)*

sticKy Talk

Use these discussion points with your group following the skit.

1. Moses had spent "quality time" with God up on the mountain, and that was when God gave him the Ten Commandments. Why is it important to spend time with God? How do you like to spend time with God?

2. God tells us honoring our parents is important in the Ten Commandments. What are ways you can honor your parents in everyday life?

3. Explain whether you think it's possible to keep all the commandments all the time.

4. Tell which commandment you think is the most difficult to keep and why. Which one is easy for you, and why? Explain whether you think one commandment is the most important and why. Which do you think we ignore the most, and why?

5. The religious leaders of the time (men who basically argued all the time) challenged Jesus to choose the most important commandment. They did this to make Jesus look bad, because whichever he chose, they thought they could argue any of the other nine. Jesus said, "I'll give you two: Love God. Love others." Describe how well you think Christians do with these two. Talk about how you live those words daily—and how you can get better at living them.

Bow to the Cow!

Almost **Instant**

Purpose: The Israelites worship a golden calf, told in an interactive and creative way.

Passage: Exodus 32:1-25

People: Narrator, Moses, Israelite, Aaron

Props:
- 2 cups
- 5 copies of the skit

Prep: Place the cups somewhere on stage where Moses can grab them at the end of the skit.

Choose four people to be the Narrator, Moses, the Israelite, and Aaron. Ask another child to control the light switch. Give everyone a copy of the skit.

Note to Director: Encourage the actors to be over the top with their motions—Aaron as he builds and then presents the idol, the Israelite as he bows, and Moses as he destroys the idol.

Narrator: *(Stands on one side of stage. Moses and the Israelite enter from opposite side.)* Moses *(Moses waves)* was the leader of the Israelites *(Israelite waves)*. Moses had led them through slavery, plagues, and doubt. And now he was leading them to the Promised Land that God had set aside for them. But first, Moses had to make a quick trip up a mountain to talk with God.

Moses: *(Waves to the Israelite and Narrator while exiting.)* I'll be right back. Don't do anything I wouldn't do.

Israelite: Of course not, Moses! For you, we'd wait a lifetime. Right, guys? *(Cues audience to respond.)*

Audience: Right!

(LIGHTS OFF)

Narrator: So they waited.

(LIGHTS ON)

Narrator: Several days passed.

(LIGHTS OFF)

Narrator: And still they waited.

(LIGHTS ON)

Narrator: And finally after 40 days…

Israelite: *(Places hands on head.)* I can't take it anymore! All this waiting. *(Looks at audience.)* Aren't you guys sick of it? Where's Moses? Does anyone see him? *(Cues audience to look around for Moses—looks left, right, up, down, and turns around.)* You know what? This is insane. I'm going to talk to Aaron. *(Walks over to Aaron, who's just entered.)*

Narrator: Aaron was Moses' brother *(Aaron waves)*, and he was in charge while Moses was gone.

Aaron: *(Looks at the Israelite.)* What's the problem, dude?

Israelite: Everyone's tired of waiting for your brother. *(Points to Aaron.)* He must've died up there or something. We can't just sit around here with nothing to worship. Why don't you whip up an idol for us?

Aaron: Like what kind of idol—a statue or something? *(Spreads arms.)* You know I'm not good at art.

Israelite: *(Shakes head.)* I don't know. But think of something. *(Throws arms in air.)* We're going cray-cray waiting for Moses!

Aaron: *(Nods head.)* All right, I'm down with it. Just let me gather some supplies. *(Shouts to audience.)* Hey, party people! Listen up! I need all your gold jewelry!

Narrator: So the Israelites gathered as much gold as they could and gave it to Aaron. Go ahead, everyone. Pretend to throw stuff at Aaron. On the count of three. One…two…three! *(Leads audience in pantomiming. Aaron acts like he's catching stuff and then building something with it.)* Once Aaron had all the gold, he threw it in a fire, melted it, and formed an idol.

Aaron: *(Stands straight and tall as if hiding something behind back.)* All right, people! You've asked for something to worship, and I've hooked you up! I give you…*(steps to the side and motions as if unveiling the finished product)* the Golden Calf!

Israelite: *(Walks over to Aaron.)* Um…dude. I don't know what you were going for, but that looks like a cow.

Aaron: It *is* a cow. Now, *bow* to the *cow*! *(Israelite bows.)*

Narrator: And so the Israelites didn't have to wait for something to worship any longer—and Aaron didn't have to hear them complaining. Everyone was pretty happy. They danced and worshipped their new god. *(Aaron and the Israelite clap and jump around.)*

Moses: *(Enters and sees the cow idol. Turns to Aaron and the Israelite and scowls.)* Aaron, that thing better not be what I think it is. *(Looks at the idol again.)* Surely it isn't. Who'd be dumb enough to make an idol in the shape of a cow?! Give me that thing! *(Pretends to shove it on the ground and stomp it to bits.)* There!

Aaron: *(Points to the Israelite.)* He made me do it! The people were going crazy waiting for you to get off that mountain! *(Motions to stomped idol bits.)* My poor cow!

Narrator: *(Shakes head.)* The Israelites had grown impatient and didn't honor God—*or* their word to Moses to wait for him. God was ready to do away with the Israelites. But Moses asked God to give them a second chance.

Bow to the Cow!

Moses: *(Looks at Aaron and the Israelite.)* You guys need to choose right now whether or not you want to repent of your sin—say you're sorry—or continue to worship things that moo! *(Grabs cups and pretends to throw bits of the idol in each one. Stirs and hands one to Aaron and one to the Israelite.)* Now drink the "MOO-LAID" and promise you'll never do this again!

Aaron and Israelite: *(Hold noses with one hand and cups with the other.)* We promise! *(Pretend to drink and make faces like it tastes bad.)*

Narrator: God forgave the Israelites. But it was a tough one to swallow.

sticky Talk

Use these discussion points with your group following the skit.

1. Moses went up the mountain and was gone for 40 days. That's a really, really long time to wait. Describe how well you wait. Explain whether you think you're an impatient person or not and why. What do you think makes time in a waiting room seem to go slower? What kinds of things do you do when you're waiting?

2. Explain whether you think there's ever a time we *should* follow the crowd. What can be good about following the crowd? What can be bad about following the crowd? Describe a time you had to decide whether to follow the crowd—what did you do, and what happened?

3. If you were walking down the street and saw a big orange sign reading "Sidewalk Closed," but you could see your destination just beyond the sign, would you walk around the sign or find a detour? Why? Explain whether you think being disobedient matters if you can see the destination before you make the choice?

4. People "bowed to the cow" because they were tired and scared and stressed and it was something they could see that felt real. The cow was solid. Explain whether you think it's hard to have faith when we can't see God. In Hebrews 11:1, the Bible says, "Faith is the confidence that what we hope for will actually happen; it gives us assurance about things we cannot see." Explain what you think this means.

Bow to the Cow!

Mr. Joshua, Tear Down That Wall!

Almost **Instant**

Purpose: The walls of Jericho fall down, as told by Joshua to the Israelite army (aka: audience).

Passage: Joshua 6

People: Joshua, Jericho, Marchers, Priests, Campers

Props:
- 2 music stands
- 3 copies of the skit
- cellophane paper, cut into pieces

Prep: Choose two people to be Joshua and Jericho and another child to control the light switch. Give each a copy of the skit.

Divide the audience into three groups— Marchers, Priests, and Campers.

Place a skit on each music stand, and place the stands on stage so actors can present like readers theater.

Note to Director: Prior to the skit, have kids practice their parts:

- Marchers—pat their legs to mimic marching sounds.
- Priests—place their fists against their mouths and make trumpet sounds.
- Campers—crackle the cellophane paper to sound like a crackling fire.

During the skit, Joshua will cue them as if they're the Israelite army.

Jericho: *(Slightly bows head.)* I'm Jericho. I'm the protector of this great city. *(Spreads arms wide.)* No one can get through my walls.

Joshua: *(Slightly bows head.)* I'm Joshua, commander of the Israelite army. *(Motions to Jericho.)* Jericho may think he's strong, but God has already given us the city. We'll fight God's way.

Jericho: *(Places fingers to lips and looks scared.)* The people in my city are scared of this little Israelite army. *(Stands straight and tall.)* But I'm not.

Joshua: *(Nods to Marchers.)* All right, Israelite army. You know what to do. God has given us this land. Now let's take it! Stay silent, speak not a word, and let's march! *(Cues Marchers to pat legs.)*

Jericho: *(Motions with both hands.)* Go ahead. Draw your swords and do your worst. You'll never get through.

Joshua: *(Nods to Priests.)* Okay, priests, time to blow your trumpets! *(Cues Priests to make trumpet sounds.)*

Jericho: Congratulations! *(Places hands on head.)* You're giving me a headache. *(Places hands on chest.)* But I'm still here.

Joshua: *(Gives a thumbs-up.)* Great job, everyone. Now let's camp for the night. Campers, let's get the campfire going. *(Cues Campers to crackle cellophane.)* Ah, I love the sound of a crackling campfire.

Jericho: *(Raises both palms.)* That's it? That's all you've got? One lap around my walls and you're going to sleep? Ha! I knew there was nothing to fear.

(LIGHTS OFF)

(LIGHTS ON)

Joshua: Wow. *(Looks up at the room lights.)* That was a quick night! *(Looks at audience.)* Good morning, troops. Today will be just like yesterday. No swords, no weapons, no speaking. Now let's march! *(Cues Marchers to pat legs.)*

Jericho: *(Looks at Joshua and then audience.)* Coming to give it one more try, are you? I hope you have a better plan.

Joshua: *(Nods to Priests.)* Priests, blow your trumpets! *(Leads Priests in making trumpet sounds.)*

Jericho: *(Motions both hands out in disgust.)* This isn't a fight; it's a parade!

Joshua: *(Gives a thumbs-up.)* Great job, Israelite army! Now let's camp for the night. *(Cues Campers to crackle cellophane.)* Sleep well because we have four more days of this, and then we give it our final blast.

(LIGHTS OFF)

Jericho: I'm bored.

(LIGHTS ON)

Jericho: I'm still bored.

Joshua: *(Claps to get everyone's attention.)* Four more days, army. We can do this.

Jericho: *(Looks incredulous.)* Four more days? I'll catch you all later. I'm going to take a nap. Wake me when it's over. *(Places chin on chest and snores softly.)*

Joshua: Let's march!
(Cues Marchers to pat legs.)
Blow the trumpets!
(Cues Priests to make trumpet sounds.)
Camp!
(Cues Campers to crackle cellophane.)

(LIGHTS OFF)

(LIGHTS ON)

Joshua: Three more. March!
(Cues Marchers to pat legs.)
Blow the trumpets!
(Cues Priests to make trumpet sounds.)
Camp!
(Cues Campers to crackle cellophane.)

(LIGHTS OFF)

(LIGHTS ON)

Joshua: Two more. March!
(Cues Marchers to pat legs.)
Blow the trumpets!
(Cues Priests to make trumpet sounds.)
Camp!
(Cues Campers to crackle cellophane.)

Mr. Joshua, Tear Down That Wall!

(LIGHTS OFF)

(LIGHTS ON)

Joshua: Last one. March!
(Cues Marchers to pat legs.)
Blow the trumpets!
(Cues Priests to make trumpet sounds.)
Camp!
(Cues Campers to crackle cellophane.)

(LIGHTS OFF)

(LIGHTS ON)

Joshua: *(Leads everyone in applause.)* Way to go, army! You made it six days!

Jericho: *(Snorts awake and then yawns.)* Yeah, way to go. Thanks for the extra sleep.

Joshua: *(Takes a deep breath in and out.)* This is it. Today's the day. We'll march around Jericho seven times. Then, after the seventh lap, we'll all shout!

Jericho: Shouting? *(Leans toward audience.)* You call yourself an army?

Joshua: *(To audience)* Get ready! March and blow the trumpets! *(Cues Marchers and Priests.)* Campers, add to the marching sounds. *(Cues Campers to join in.)* Come on, and don't stop until I tell you. One…two…three… four…five…six…seven. Now everyone shout! *(Motions for everyone to shout and raises hands higher and higher to raise the volume. After a few seconds of shouting, cues everyone to stop.)*

Jericho: *(Places hand on forehead.)* What's happening? I don't feel so good. *(Falls to the ground.)*

Joshua: *(Leads everyone in clapping again.)* We did it! The land of Jericho is ours and all the treasures and food there too. Nothing and no one is too strong for God.

Jericho: *(Lifts head up.)* Help, I've fallen and I can't get up. *(Drops head back down.)*

Joshua: What a glorious victory for us! God provided for us in a truly miraculous way. *(Exits, dragging Jericho offstage.)*

Use these discussion points with your group following the skit.

1. Give an example of the loudest noise you can make by yourself. (Allow a few attempts.) If you really, really needed to get someone's attention, you'd probably shout very loudly. Describe what you do when you hear thunder far away. Explain how that's different from when you hear thunder up close. Why do you think we choose to listen to some things and ignore other things? Explain whether you think we ignore God at times and why.

2. Give a definition of the word *instant*. Name as many things as you can that are instant. (Allow one minute.) Explain what *instant* means to you today. Explain whether you think the old phrase "Good things come to those who wait" is true. Why or why not? Describe some things that are worth waiting for. Why do you think God made Joshua wait?

3. How well do you think you follow instructions? Explain whether you typically do something new until you get the hang of it or you read all the instructions first. Why? Tell about a situation in which following the instructions is the best thing to do. Tell about a situation in which it's best to make it up as you go along. Why do you think it's important for us to follow God's instructions?

4. Explain whether you think God allows variation from his instructions. Do you think God changes his mind? Why or why not? Which is more important: the end result or the journey to get there—and why?

Throwdown Showdown

Purpose: The battle between David and Goliath is told as a western showdown.

Passage: 1 Samuel 17

People: Cowboy (or Cowgirl) Narrator

Props:

- crumpled sheet of scrap paper (1 wad per person)

- 1 copy of the skit

Prep: Choose someone to be the Cowboy (or Cowgirl) Narrator— you could do it if you'd like! Give each child a wad of paper to throw at the appointed time during the skit.

Note to Director: Encourage the Narrator to read the entire script in a cowboy drawl and have fun with it!

Narrator: *(Enters from side of stage, placing hands on hips and walking as if with spurs on boots.)* Ching, ching, ching…*(Looks at audience.)* That's the sound of my spurs on my boots. *(Takes a few more steps.)* Ching, ching, ching…*(Looks at audience again.)* I love the sound of these spurs!

(Faces audience.) Howdy, y'all! How many of you young'uns have heard about David and Goliath? *(Pauses.)* Well, I'm not surprised one bit, 'cause it's a powerful part of the Bible! Now, how many of you know how to make noise? *(Pauses.)* Well, that doesn't surprise me either, 'cause y'all are a bunch of rascals! So I guess you won't mind helping me out for the next bit of time by bein' a little bit rowdy, would ya? *(Pauses.)* Okay then, let's roll like a tumbleweed on the prairie! Now, I know David and Goliath lived a long time ago—before there were cowboys, pistols, and such. But if you ask me, this here was a showdown! And bein' as I'm a cowboy, that's how I'm gonna tell it.

(Takes a deep breath and then clears throat.) Now, the Israelites were dealing with a bunch of bad guys called the Philistines. The Philistines were about as mean and nasty as they come. And there was this one fella in the bunch named Goliath. He was one tall drink of water. When Goliath walked, it sounded like a herd of buffalo. *(Cues audience.)* Let me hear you stomp your feet.

Audience: *(Stomps feet.)*

Narrator: *(Nods head.)* Yep. That's what it sounded like when giant Goliath walked around. He also had a big, fat mouth to boot. He kept pickin' on the Israelites with fightin' words. You see, the Israelites and the Philistines were in a fight and were lined up across from each other in a valley. Every day at sunup, Goliath would come out and tease the Israelites, laughin' as they were shakin' in their boots. He'd say, "One of you yellow bellies come out and fight me!" *(Cues audience.)* Let me hear you say those words!

Audience: One of you yellow bellies come out and fight me!

Narrator: *(Shakes head.)* Well, that Goliath was so mean that he kept on hollerin' and hollerin' every mornin' for 40 days, and the Israelites were just about fed up! But it just so happened that David, who'd been watchin' sheep back home, had been sent by his daddy to fetch some vittles for his brothers who were fightin' in the feud. David asked his brothers, "Now what's all that ruckus?" *(Cues audience.)* Say it with me…

Audience: Now what's all that ruckus?

Narrator: So the Israelites told David what was goin' on. One of David's brothers got a burr under his hat about it. *(Shakes finger as if confronting David.)* The brother told David to mind his own business and get back to his sheep wranglin'. *(Cues audience.)* Let me see you wrangle and round up some sheep. While you're at it, sound off like a bunch of sheep too!

Audience: *(Pretending to herd sheep.)* Baa!

Narrator: *(Shakes head.)* But David wouldn't stand for it, and pretty soon Saul, the head honcho of the Israelite army, got wind of David bein' amongst the ranks. *(Places both hands on hips.)* So Saul went to have a word with David. *(Bows slightly.)* David told him, "Don't you worry one bit. I'll get that overgrown ape and teach him a thing or two!" Saul told David he was crazier than a bag of raccoons! But David said, "I ain't scared!" *(Cues audience.)* Now you say it…

Audience: I ain't scared!

Narrator: Then David told Saul how he arm wrestled lions and bears just for fun. *(Moves arms as if wrestling an animal.)* So Saul said, "Go on then, and God bless ya!" *(Raises hand high as if in blessing.)* Saul tried to give David some fancy weapons to kill Goliath, but David wouldn't have any part of that *(shakes head)*. David was good with rocks, so rocks are what he'd use. Meanwhile big Goliath *(raises arms high)* got a good look at little David *(moves arms low)* and had himself a good chuckle. *(Cues audience.)* Let me hear you chuckle like Goliath…

Audience: *(Chuckles like Goliath.)*

Narrator: Goliath was *huge!* *(Cues audience.)* So let me hear a *huge* chuckle!

Audience: *(Makes huge, loud chuckle.)*

Narrator: Goliath said, "Those Israelites are off their lovin' rockers! That boy ain't no taller than a goat!" But those would be the last words Goliath spoke. Because David picked up one of his rocks, put it in his trusty slingshot and started twirlin' it *(pretends to twirl slingshot)* above his head. *(Cues audience.)* Lemme see you twirl a slingshot…

Audience: *(Pretends to twirl slingshots.)*

Narrator: Next thing you know, that rock came a-flyin' out of that sling like a two-fanged bat and hit Goliath *(smacks forehead)* right smack in the middle of his noggin! *(Cues audience.)* Why don't you give it a try? Throw them paper wads like you was slinging rocks.

Audience: *(Throws paper wads.)*

Throwdown Showdown

Narrator: That big boy's mouth was finally shut up three ways to Sunday! The Israelites had won the fight! Yee-haw! *(Cues audience.)* Say it with me now…

Audience: Yee-haw!

Narrator: *(Waves to audience.)* Good job, people. Time for me to mosey on home. *(Exits, making spur sounds.)* Ching, ching, ching…*(Looks at audience one more time before moving out of sight.)* Y'all take care now. Ya hear?

Use these discussion points with your group following the skit.

1. Goliath was so big and so mean and so full of himself that he was very intimidating. People didn't even try to fight him because they knew there was no point; they would lose. Explain whether you think there's anything in the world today that seems like a battle not worth fighting and why. Tell about a time you faced something that seemed impossible and did it anyway.

2. David selected five smooth stones from the stream to take into his battle with the giant. He probably took his time selecting the right stones. Think about a big problem in your life right now. What are five "stones" you could use to help you face your problem?

3. Before he defeated Goliath, David was kind of like a street musician for King Saul. He could play his harp and help the king's tormenting spirit go away. Describe at least one of your special talents. (Encourage every child to name at least one talent.) How can you use your special talent to help someone? In what ways could you use your talent for God?

4. What would you say to God before walking out onto a battlefield like David did?

Under the Big Top: Daniel the Great!

Purpose: Daniel in the lions' den is told by the master of ceremonies of a big-top circus. Kids will learn that there are no "tricks or performances" necessary when dealing with problems; the greatest thing you can do is pray!

Passage: Daniel 6

People: Daniel, Master of Ceremonies, 2 Trainers, Lions

Props:

- 2 hula hoops
- microphone (or pretend with a comb or wooden spoon)
- 2 beach balls
- 1 copy of the skit

Prep: You can be Master of Ceremonies (or choose another volunteer to). Ask someone to be Daniel and two others to be Trainers. Give each Trainer a hula hoop and beach ball. Some of the audience will be the Lions.

Notes to Director:

- Daniel has three lines. You could write these lines on index cards for him to read and it'd be funny—he wouldn't need a script.

- Before the skit, see which kids know how to somersault or cartwheel. During the skit, the Trainers will have some Lions do those stunts. When kids are called to "jump through the hoop," they'll hold the hoop and use it like a jump rope. If kids don't want to do any of the previous stunts, they could catch and toss balls when it's time during the skit. Or if they don't want to do any of the stunts, they can be the audience and applaud when cued.

MC: (Walks onstage and spreads arms wide.) Ladies and gentlemen, it's the moment you've all been waiting for—the big finish to our magnificent circus show! Let's give a big round of applause for the lions! (Leads audience in applause.)

Just wanted to give you a heads-up that the lions are getting warmed up and ready to pounce out into the crowd and eat you alive! (Pauses.) Just kidding! The lions are tame. I'll show you why they're tame in just a few minutes. But first, let's see a few tricks from these kings of the jungle! Our trainers have been working hard to give you a great show tonight. Let's give them a little encouragement, folks! Give it up for Dillweed and Soy! (Leads audience in applause.)

(TRAINERS ENTER FROM OPPOSITE SIDES OF THE STAGE. EACH CARRIES A HULA HOOP AND BEACH BALL.)

MC: All right, I think our trainers are ready. (Nods to Trainers.) Our lions are ready. (Nods to Lions.) Okay, now before we begin, I must tell you that these tricks are special. They represent a hero from the Bible. I'm going to tell you about Daniel while the lions perform. Daniel lived away from home. He believed in our one true God. Everyone else around him didn't believe in God.

The lions will help us along the way as we learn about Daniel. Now, for their first trick, some lions are going to do a somersault or front roll. This represents 120 governors who *rolled* into the palace of a king named Darius. The governors—or leaders—were jealous of Daniel and wanted to get him in trouble. Lions, show us how you roll!

(TRAINERS MOTION FOR LIONS TO COME FORWARD AND SOMERSAULT OR FRONT ROLL AND THEN LEAD EVERYONE IN APPLAUSE.)

MC: Next, our lions are going to do a trick that is stand-out sensational, just like a man named Daniel in the Bible. Daniel didn't just roll into the palace; he did a cartwheel! Lions, put your paws up!

(TRAINERS MOTION FOR LIONS TO COME FORWARD AND DO A CARTWHEEL AND THEN LEAD EVERYONE IN APPLAUSE.)

MC: Just kidding! Daniel didn't cartwheel, but he was very, very brave. And he totally trusted God in a hard time. (Shakes head.) The governors didn't like Daniel's performance. In fact, they jumped through hoops to find a way to get rid of him. Lions, hoop it up!

(TRAINERS MOTION FOR LIONS TO COME FORWARD AND USE HULA HOOPS LIKE JUMP ROPES AND THEN LEAD EVERYONE IN APPLAUSE.)

MC: Upon being tricked into it, King Darius, who loved Daniel, had no choice but to throw Daniel into a den full of…wait for it…*lions*! Lions, go deep!

(TRAINERS THROW BEACH BALLS TO LIONS IN AUDIENCE, WHO THROW THEM BACK AND PASS BACK AND FORTH FOR SEVERAL SECONDS. THEN TRAINERS LEAD EVERYONE IN APPLAUSE.)

MC: I bet you're wondering how that turned out for Daniel. Would you like to know? *(Nods head up and down and cues audience to respond.)*

Audience: Yes!

MC: *(Places both hands on head.)* Well, hold on to your hats, folks, because I have a big surprise for you! You may think Daniel was turned into ground taco meat. But he's here with us today! Ladies and gentlemen, give a nice big welcome to Daniel the Great! *(Leads audience in applause as Daniel enters. Puts arm around Daniel.)* Now I understand that you did something special in that lions' den—which is why you're here with us today and not ground taco meat.

Daniel: *(Nods head.)* Yes, I did.

MC: I also know from the Bible that this is the very special thing that caused you *(motions to Daniel)* to be thrown into that den in the first place.

Daniel: *(Nods head.)* Yes, it is.

MC: Well, then would it be possible for you to show us?

Daniel: *(Nods head again.)* Yes, it would.

MC: All right, ladies and gentlemen! Here to perform the act that was important enough to have him thrown to his death and to somehow save his life, I give you *(motions to Daniel again)* Daniel the Great!

Daniel: *(Drops into prayer position on knees.)*

MC: Ladies and gentlemen, there you have it! The power of prayer! *(Cues audience.)* Let's give Daniel a *roar*!

Audience: Roar!

(MC HELPS DANIEL UP; THEN MC, DANIEL, AND TRAINERS WAVE AS THEY EXIT.)

Under the Big Top: Daniel the Great!

Use these discussion points with your group following the skit.

1. Describe where you most like to pray. Describe what you're most likely to pray for: solutions, strength, patience, protection, or comfort. Since prayer is a conversation, describe what you think God says back to you.

2. Bowing our heads and folding our hands is an accepted prayer position. Some people pray with their hands in the air. Some pray in other positions. Describe what you think would happen if you prayed standing on one foot with one finger touching the end of your nose and your eyes open.

3. Tell about a situation in which you think doing the right thing might not be the safe thing. Describe whether your faith has ever gotten you in trouble. Explain whether you've lost friends because of your beliefs. What happened? Explain whether you've ever lost a friend because of his or her beliefs.

4. Tell about a time God worked through you to reach out and tell someone else about him. What happened?

5. God gives us many gifts. Sometimes being a good listener is a gift from God. What do you think some of Daniel's gifts were? Tell about other people in the Bible who had similar gifts. What gifts do you believe God has given you? Explain whether you think we have a responsibility to use the gifts God has given us.

Opposite Day

Purpose: Jonah's adventure is told from the perspective of the Big Fish. Kids will learn that disobedience affects others and has huge consequences, but God is always faithful and wants us to learn from our mistakes.

Passage: Jonah 1:1–4:11

People: Big Fish (Narrator)

Props:
- 1 copy of the skit

Prep: You can be the Big Fish (Narrator) or ask another volunteer to.

Note to Director: Before the skit, tell kids, "The word *opposite* means 'backward' or 'different from what you thought.' When something in the skit is backward or different, you'll be cued to shout 'Opposite Day!' " Practice the response a couple of times by pointing to the kids and having them shout "Opposite Day!"

Big Fish: *(Enters from side of stage and waves to audience.)* Hello. I'd introduce myself to you with a name, but the Bible just calls me the Big Fish. I gotta tell ya, I've heard some pretty goofy names in the Bible, so I'm actually kinda glad I'm not called one like "Mushi" or "Puah." *(Pauses and takes a deep breath.)* Anyhoo, there's this guy in the Bible named Jonah. Nice guy...a little stubborn. What you may not know is that Jonah started a little thing I call "Opposite Day."

(Places hands behind ears.) Now I know fish don't have ears—which is probably why nobody ever asked me to tell my side of Jonah's experience—but I heard the whole thing. Of course, I was underwater when the whole thing happened, so I didn't actually *see* much. I want you to help me relive the experience because it's without a doubt the most exciting thing that could happen to a smelly fish like me!

(Motions with both arms out wide.) It all started when God told Jonah, "Go to Ninevah!" From underwater it kinda sounded like God had his face in a bowl of JELL-O. *(Cues audience.)* Say "Go to Ninevah" for me, and let me see if you know what I mean.

Audience: Go to Ninevah!

Big Fish: *(Nods head.)* That's about right. But I don't think it sounded like that to Jonah. I think Jonah heard God loud and clear, only he didn't go to Ninevah. He did the opposite. Again—nice guy, kinda stubborn. Jonah must've thought it was...*(Points to audience.)*

Audience: Opposite Day!

Big Fish: You betcha. So instead of going to Ninevah, Jonah hops a boat to Tarshish. *(Shakes head.)* Now, you've probably heard the term "smooth sailing," but God had other ideas for that boat—because Jonah disobeyed. It wasn't smooth sailing at all because it was... *(Points to audience.)*

Audience: Opposite Day!

Big Fish: *(Nods head.)* Toot sweet! That boat was rocking all over the place because the wind was a hot mess! You'd think that every single person on that boat would be completely freaked out—as most of them were. All except Jonah, who was down in the bottom of the boat...wait for it...*sleeping*! Sleeping and dreaming that it was... *(Points to audience.)*

Audience: Opposite Day!

Big Fish: *(Nods head.)* Ding, ding, ding! To make matters worse, as the sea got rougher and rougher, people started getting sick from all the commotion in the ocean. So they started hurling everywhere! It was a disgusting sound. *(Cues audience.)* Let me hear that sound...

Audience: *(Makes sound of throwing up.)*

Big Fish: Okay, wow. *(Looks disgusted.)* You must've done that before. Anyhoo, being in the middle of the ocean like that with the gnarly waves crashing all around you, you'd probably be hanging on to that boat for dear life. But Jonah could not. Because of his disobedience, the other passengers had no choice but to throw Jonah into the raging sea. They didn't want to do it. But it was...*(Points to audience.)*

Audience: Opposite Day!

Big Fish: *(Nods head again.)* You get the picture. But chucking Jonah into the water totally solved the problem. The sea went from "electric Chihuahua" mode to "lie like broccoli" mode. Let me see you go crazy and then chill...*(Leads audience.)*

Audience: *(Acts crazy and then completely calm.)*

Big Fish: *(Does a double take at audience.)* Okay, you guys need to eat less sugar. Anyhoo, this is my favorite part! I was swimming along, minding my own beeswax *(makes swimming motions)* when all of a sudden my mouth opens up *(opens mouth and says the rest of the line with mouth open)* and Jonah swims right into my belly! *(Places both hands on stomach.)* I've been scared of humans all my life because, well, who likes being tricked into chomping down on a sharp, hooked piece of metal? *(Places index finger into mouth like a hook.)* But instead of a human catching me, *I* caught a human! Because it was...*(Points to audience.)*

Audience: Opposite Day!

Big Fish: Righty-o! Now, normally when you tickle a belly, it's from the outside. *(Tickles belly and laughs a bit.)* But, once again, this was...*(Points to audience.)*

Audience: Opposite Day!

Big Fish: *(Nods head.)* Uh-huh. So Jonah tickled me around from the *inside* for three days. *(Rubs belly.)* Jonah also did a lot of praying. He offered God a big apology, said a big thank-you, and admitted he'd learned a big lesson—all while being inside this Big Fish! Then God told me in his JELL-O voice, "Spit Jonah out!" *(Cues audience.)* Let me hear you say that.

Opposite Day

Audience: Spit Jonah out!

Big Fish: So for the second time since you've been listening—bleh! *(Pantomimes throwing up.)* And I'm not sure if you know just how gross it is to see this Big Fish blow chunks, but maybe you can show me...*(Cues audience.)*

Audience: *(Pretends to throw up like the Big Fish.)*

Big Fish: *(Motions with both hands out.)* Wow. I don't want to be around when one of you gets sick. Anyhoo, if you want some advice from this Big Fish—because I know you do—do what God tells you the first time!

Use these discussion points with your group following the skit.

1. Think about the longest car ride you've ever endured. Describe some ways you passed the time. Years ago, there were no DVD players or music players in cars and no hand-held video games. We have it pretty comfortable these days. Try to imagine what Jonah's travel might have been like inside the great fish. It would have been pretty awful, and Jonah had a lot of time to think about things. Explain whether you think what happened to Jonah was like or unlike what happens when you get grounded by parents or a timeout at school.

2. A wise man once said, "God will speak to you in one of two ways. He will whisper in your ear or he will hit you upside the head with a brick." Talk about a time God whispered in your ear. Now talk about a time God hit you upside the head with a brick. Describe what it's like to know God is telling you something.

3. Tell about what you think happens when God's plan isn't exactly your plan for what should happen. Explain whether you think God bargains and why. Even if God never sets a giant task before you, he may ask little things of you every day. Talk about some of the little things God asks us to do. In your opinion, what's the hardest part about being faithful to God?

4. Explain whether you think having an "everything is going my way" day means God is happy with you. What if you're having a "nothing is going right today" day? Explain whether you think you can tell if God is happy or unhappy with you.

Jack in the Box

Purpose: Jack the Donkey tells about Jesus' birth as well as interesting facts about his species. In a book of sticky skits, this one gives kids something to hold on to that they might not have known before!

Passage: Luke 2:1-20

People: Jack the Donkey

Props:
- 1 copy of the skit

Prep: Choose a male volunteer to be Jack the Donkey. Since this is a monologue, the actor can read the script.

Note to Director: Instruct the actor to know the script well enough so he can have eye contact with the audience.

Jack the Donkey: *(Enters from side of stage and talks to audience.)* Hi! My name is Jack the Donkey. When Jesus was born, there wasn't any nice room for him to stay in, so his mom laid him in a manger, which is a wooden box that animals eat from. I was right beside that manger. So you might say I was the first "Jack in the Box" at Christmas! *(Nods head and acknowledges audience is listening.)* All male donkeys are called Jack, by the way.

(Places hands on chest.) My Christmas journey started in Nazareth. At this time, Jesus hadn't been born yet…but his birth was really close. Mary and Joseph needed my help traveling from there to Bethlehem so they could register for a census. A census is where all the people are counted. *(Tilts head.)* Weird, right? Anyway…*(stands straight and flexes muscles)* for their size, donkeys are stronger than horses, so I was able to carry Mary on my back for a long distance with no problem. (Even though Mary was also carrying a special load herself.) You know, most people look down on us donkeys because, well, we are short. *(Motions with both hands down low.)* So you literally have to look down. But it would've been much harder for Mary to get on and off a tall horse with that baby in her belly!

It took at least four days *(holds up four fingers)* for us to get to Bethlehem. I bet you would've packed lots of snacks for your belly on such a long trip! Especially in that dry land without any convenience stores! *(Motions with both hands out.)* But I can eat almost any kind of plant I find, and I did just fine eating what grew in the desert.

(Wipes sweat from forehead.) When we finally got through the desert to Bethlehem, there was no place for Mary and Joseph to stay inside. The best place available was a small place with a manger. This was fine by me. *(Nods head.)* I was happy to be with other animals because donkeys don't like to be alone. I get along great with sheep and goats. So I was happy to be in a place where there were other animals hanging around. I'm protective in nature *(punches fists)* and would guard baby Jesus and the other animals if given the chance.

Not too long after we got there, Jesus was born. *(Holds arms as if rocking a baby.)* Some shepherds were nearby when an angel came to them. It scared the shepherds something fierce! *(Looks scared.)* But the angel told them not to be afraid, for he was bringing good news that'd cause great joy to all people! *(Looks happy.)* A Savior, the Messiah, had been born! They could find him wrapped snugly in cloths, lying in a manger. *(Motions with arms wide overhead.)* Then a bunch of other heavenly hosts appeared with the angel, shouting, "Glory to God in highest heaven, and peace on earth to those with whom God is pleased!"

(Leans toward audience as if giving important news.) Now, speaking of scared, I must let you know something else about us donkeys. We don't scare as easily as horses. We're also very intelligent. *(Runs in place.)* Instead of running away from danger like horses tend to do, we'll run down a predator or make him go away with a strong, well-aimed kick! *(Kicks one leg.)*

(Stands straight and takes a deep breath.) But back to the baby Jesus! The shepherds made their way to Bethlehem to find Jesus. They found him just as the angels had told them, lying in the manger. *(Places both hands to side of head.)* The shepherds were so excited and went out to spread the word about Jesus. They told the good news to all who'd hear! (Donkeys can hear each other from up to 60 miles away, FYI!)

(Takes a bow.) Thank you for letting me tell you about Jesus' birth! I bet you thought I could only say "Heehaw!" *(Motions to audience.)* Do as the shepherds did and spread the good news of Jesus with everyone! *(Waves as exiting.)* God wants everyone to know about his Son, Jesus!

Jack in the Box

Use these discussion points with your group following the skit.

1. There are all kinds of stories and legends about the birth of Jesus. There are stories about talking animals and drummer boys and lost wise men. The real event, though, is pretty simple. Explain whether you've ever been in a Christmas pageant and what part you played. Why do you think we work so hard to re-enact Jesus' birth? Describe something you think might've happened in the stable that nobody has ever talked about.

2. Most of us have heard the events surrounding Jesus' birth over and over since we were very small children. But imagine you met someone from a faraway place who'd never heard of Jesus. How would you tell his story?

3. Why do you think God told only the shepherds—and not everyone—about Jesus' birth?

4. Joseph doesn't usually get many good lines in plays about Christmas. Sometimes it's hard to tell him apart from the shepherds in the Nativity sets we display each Christmas. Think about what would be the best line for Joseph to say about Jesus' birth, and then share with the group.

Almost **Instant**

Best Neighbor Ever!

Purpose: The parable of the Good Samaritan is told by the TV show "Best Neighbor Ever!"

Passage: Luke 10:30-37

People: Host, Man, 3 others (who'll play 3 Robbers and then the Priest, Levite, and Samaritan)

Props:
- 5 copies of the skit

Prep: You could be the Host (or ask another volunteer to). Choose four others to be the Man, Priest, Levite, and Samaritan. Give each person a copy of the script.

Note to Director: You can keep this skit Almost Instant by using no props—simply have actors pantomime. Or you can boost the skit to Percolator and include the following props:

- microphone for the Host
- paper towel tubes (for sticks)
- bag (for stealing)
- Bible for the Priest
- gold-foil-wrapped candy coins
- paper money
- adhesive bandages

Host: *(Enters from side of stage.)* Welcome, welcome, welcome! It's time for another episode of everyone's favorite game show—"Best Neighbor Ever!" I'm your Host, and here with me are *(spreads arms wide)* all of you! Thanks for being here to play today!

Okay, so let's get started. Here's how the game goes. I'm going to bring on four potential neighbors for you to meet. Your job is to pick which of the four neighbors is the Best…Neighbor…Ever! *(Cues audience.)* Say it with me…

Audience: Best…Neighbor…Ever!

Host: Who's ready?

Man: *(Enters from side. Waves hand at Host and audience.)* I'm ready! *(Stops at center stage.)*

Host: Excellent. Let's get started. Let's say you're walking down the road. *(Man starts walking in place.)* You're by yourself. Time to meet our first contestants, who call themselves the Robbers. Let's see what kind of neighbors they'll be.

Robbers: *(Come out; pantomime hitting Man, taking his money, and sticking it in their bag; and then run offstage. Man lies on the floor.)*

Host: Oh no! The Robbers attacked him and stole his money. Do the Robbers seem like the Best Neighbors Ever? *(Shakes head and cues audience to respond.)*

Audience: No!

Host: Let's move on to our next contestant. This contestant calls himself the Priest. Let's see what kind of neighbor the Priest will be!

Priest: *(Enters and notices Man on the ground. Man groans in pain. Priest looks at him, looks around, and hurries on by.)*

Host: *(Looks amazed.)* Did you see that? The Priest did nothing! He just ignored him. Does the Priest seem like the Best Neighbor Ever? *(Shakes head and cues audience to respond.)*

Audience: No!

Host: *(Keeps shaking head.)* Let's move on to our next contestant. This contestant calls himself the Levite. Let's see what kind of neighbor the Levite will be!

Levite: *(Enters, looks at Man groaning in pain on the ground, looks around, and hurries on by.)*

Host: *(Opens mouth wide in shock.)* Did you see that? The Levite did the exact same thing as the Priest. *Nothing!* He just ignored him. Does the Levite seem like the Best Neighbor Ever? *(Shakes head and cues audience to respond.)*

Audience: No!

Host: *(Shakes head in disbelief.)* Let's move on to our last contestant. This contestant calls himself the Samaritan. Let's see what kind of neighbor the Samaritan will be!

Samaritan: *(Enters, notices the Man, hurries over to him, pantomimes bandaging him and giving him money, and helps him up and offstage.)*

Host: *(Looks happily amazed.)* Did you see that? The Samaritan helped the Man. He bandaged him, gave him money to take care of himself, and helped him off to get more help. Does the Samaritan seem like the Best Neighbor Ever? *(Nods head up and down and cues audience to respond.)*

Audience: Yes!

Host: There you have it! *(Spreads arms wide.)* The Samaritan wins the prize of, say it with me…*(Leads audience in shouting.)*

Audience: Best…Neighbor…Ever!

Best Neighbor Ever!

Use these discussion points with your group following the skit.

1. Tell about a time you stopped what you were doing to help someone, even though it cost you time or money or the opportunity to do something else. Describe how knowing it would "cost" you to help the person made you feel. Now tell about a time someone stopped what he or she was doing to help you. Describe what that experience felt like.

2. The priest and the Levite both might have had perfectly acceptable reasons they didn't stop to help the injured man. Some were deeply held religious reasons. Tell about a time you found a good reason to not help someone when you could have. How was that situation like or unlike what happened in this parable?

3. Jesus told this story purposefully to a group of people who hated Samaritans. Tell about a time you were wrong about a person or a group of people. Describe what happened that made you change your mind about them.

4. This story, like a lot of Jesus' stories, doesn't have a definite ending. We don't know what happened to the injured man, the man who helped, or the robbers. Explain why you think Jesus leaves us with unanswered questions.

Camp Lost-a-Lot

Purpose: The Parable of the Lost Sheep is told by a camp counselor looking for a lost camper. This skit will help kids realize each one of them is important to God. God pursues them and isn't willing for any one of them to remain lost.

Passage: Luke 15:1-7

People: Camp Leader, Campers, Tyler

Props:
- clipboard
- 1 copy of the skit

Prep: Choose someone to be the Camp Leader—have him or her talk in a southern drawl. The audience will be the Campers. Choose a boy to be Tyler, and have him hide behind something in the room during the skit. Only the Camp Leader will know where he's hiding. Wherever he hides will be where the "big rock" is during the skit. Tyler will stay hidden until the end of the skit when he hears his cue, pops out, and says "Here I am!"

Note to Director: Place a copy of the skit on a clipboard. The Camp Leader can hold it and use it as a reference.

Camp Leader: *(Enters from side of stage, holding clipboard. Checks clipboard, and then looks up and waves.)* Hey, y'all! Your friendly Camp Leader here, getting ready for roll call! *(Looks at clipboard.)* Okay, Janie…*(Looks up and then motions as if seeing Janie.)* Check! *(Looks at clipboard.)* Tyler… *(Looks up.)* Tyler? Tyyyy-lerrrr? *(Looks down at clipboard and then back up.)* Well, I'll be a graham cracker. Not again!

(Motions to audience.) Have y'all seen Tyler? I told him not to play ninja woods warrior anymore…*(Turns around as if looking for Tyler.)* All righty…I need to go look for that little whipper snapper, and I'm *not* going back into those spooky woods by myself! *(Motions to audience again.)* I need your help, fellow campers! *(Has audience stand up.)* Come on, let's giddy up!

(Leads audience in walking in place, exaggerated and silly. Then stops walking.) Okay, now this here hill is a booger. But we gotta get to the top so we can get a good look. So make like a monkey and let's get movin'! *(Leads audience in pretending to climb to the top of the hill.)* I really shoulda stopped myself after that third s'more! *(Leads audience in more climbing and then stops.)* Okay, whew! Finally made it!

Let's see if Tyler's 'round here somewhere…*(Leads audience in looking for Tyler. Places hand above eyes, looks left, right, up, down, and turns around.)* I don't see hide nor hair of him here. This calls for our special Camp Lost-a-Lot findin' call! I'm gonna teach it to you! Ready? *(Puts hands around mouth.)* Cock-a-doodle-lahee-hoooo! *(Cues audience to join in.)* Come on, y'all! Help a feller out here!

Audience: Cock-a-doodle-lahee-hoooo!

Camp Leader: *(Cups hands behind ears.)* Y'all hear anything? *(Pauses.)* Aw, marshmellers. I don't hear a peep. Let's keep movin.' *(Motions for audience to walk in place and then stops.)* Oh boy. The creek. I hope that crazy beaver doesn't see me this time! I don't need another hole in my short pants! *(Places one hand on back pocket as if to feel a hole.)* We have to use one of his logs to get across. Let's hurry 'fore he catches us—but watch you don't fall in that water! It's colder than a snowman's hug! *(Puts arms straight out to sides and pretends to balance while walking. Motions for audience to do the same.)*

Okey-dokey! Here we are! *(Stops balancing and looks around. Talks again in a whisper.)* The woods. Now stay close. This place is creepier than an old man's toenails! Get out your binoculars so we can get a better look-see. *(Leads audience in putting hands into two circles as "binoculars" up to eyes. Looks side to side.*

Stops suddenly, jumps back, and yells.) Ahhhh!

(Points ahead.) Did you see that? That looks like Chewbacca! *(Looks into binoculars again and then puts them back down.)* Well, I'll be! You know—a caterpillar that close up looks just like Big Foot's finger! I don't see a thing. I reckon we better try callin' Tyler again. *(Takes a deep breath and then yells.)* Cock-a-doodle-lahee-hoooo! *(Cues audience.)* Say it with me!

Audience: Cock-a-doodle-lahee-hoooo!

Camp Leader: Well, chocolate bars. *(Shakes head.)* Tyler's not here either. There's just one more place to look...behind that big rock over there. *(Points into distance.)* It's gettin' awful dark out here, and we still gotta make our way back to camp. We better hightail it! Let's run! *(Leads audience in being goofy and running in place. Then stops and yells again.)* Tyler! You here, boy? Tyyyy-lerrrr! If you're around, say in your best robot voice *(or whatever accent you so choose)* "Here I am."

Tyler: *(Pops up and responds in robot voice.)* Here I am!

Camp Leader: *(Startled)* Jumpin' roasted hot dogs! There you are! Let's get ourselves back to camp! I reckon since we found you, we can have a little treat when we get there! Everyone, rejoice with me! We found Tyler! *(Leads audience in cheering.)*

(Places arm around Tyler.) You see, Tyler, even though I may have 100 campers here, if I lose one of them, I go out of my way to find that lost camper and bring that one home. Now let's get back to camp and make some s'mores! I'm hungry. Thanks for helping me look, everybody.

Tyler: *(Waves to audience and talks in robot voice.)* Thank you!

Camp Lost-a-Lot

sticKy Talk

Use these discussion points with your group following the skit.

1. Describe what you think would happen if you lost your pen at school. What if you lost your lunch money? What about if you lost your homework that was due that day? Would you search for those things with the same intensity? Why or why not? How does it feel to know we're all equally valued by Jesus?

2. Sometimes playing Hide-and-Go-Seek is really more like playing Hide-and-Go-Listen. If you listen, you can hear where people are hiding without having to seek them. Tell whether you've ever tried to hide from God. What are ways we try to hide from God?

3. There's an old song that says, "I once was lost, but now am found." In the song, it's God's grace that is doing the seeking. Explain what you think grace is. How does God's grace find us? Why do you think God's grace can always find us, no matter how well we hide?

4. Many people are wandering, and they might not even be aware that they are. Do you think Jesus searches for people even when they don't yet know they're lost? Why or why not? What does this parable tell you about how Jesus feels about his sheep?

How Low Can You Go, Zacchaeus?

Purpose: A skit about Zacchaeus is combined with a Limbo game. This "short" story teaches a "big" lesson about how Jesus' influence can change hearts!

Passage: Luke 19:1-10

People: Narrator

Props:
- Limbo pole (or broomstick)
- 1 copy of the skit

Prep: You can be the Narrator (or choose another volunteer to). Ask two kids to hold the Limbo pole. Children will play the Limbo game, going under the pole after each cue by the Narrator. The pole will lower each time. Alternate pole-holders so everyone gets a chance to Limbo!

Note to Director: Prior to the skit, practice the Limbo as well as audience responses. So much fun!

(TWO KIDS WALK TO CENTER STAGE, HOLDING THE LIMBO POLE HIGH.)

Narrator: *(Stands close by.)* The streets of Jericho were hopping like crazy! Jesus was coming through, and everyone was so happy! As people made their way into the street, they shouted and danced: "Whoop! Whoop!" *(Clap! Clap!)* "Whoop! Whoop!" *(Motions for audience to come forward and Limbo as they shout and clap.)*

Audience: Whoop! Whoop! *(Clap! Clap!)* Whoop! Whoop!

Narrator: Now, there was this dude named Zacchaeus. Today he might be nicknamed "Z-Money" because he was the boss—and he was loaded with green! But he had no friends because he was also a cheat. It was his job to collect taxes, but he liked to skim a little for himself, so he charged a little extra. The people said, "No-no, Zacchaeus! That's low-low, Zacchaeus!" *(Kids lower the Limbo pole. Narrator motions for others to come forward and Limbo as they shout.)*

Audience: No-no, Zacchaeus! That's low-low, Zacchaeus!

Narrator: That Zacchaeus was not a really nice guy. *(Shakes head.)* And to make it worse, he was a shorty. This definitely did *not* help his attitude. So he got pretty irritated when the crowd blocked his view of Jesus coming through. He ran ahead of the crowd, found a sycamore-fig tree, and used some mad climbing skills! He was up that tree as quick as a monkey! The crowd shouted: "Ooh-ooh! Ah-ah! Ooh-ooh! Ah-ah!" *(Kids lower the Limbo pole. Narrator motions for others to come forward and Limbo as they shout.)*

Audience: Ooh-ooh! Ah-ah! Ooh-ooh! Ah-ah!

Narrator: Jesus came to the spot in the road where the tree was. *(Looks up.)* He looked up, saw Zacchaeus, and told him to get out of that tree toot-quick! *(Motions "come here.")* And then Jesus told Zacchaeus he wanted to crash at his crib. Zacchaeus thought that was pretty sweet! So he climbed down and started walking with Jesus to his house. The crowd began to mumble: "No, Jesus, no! You really shouldn't go! No, Jesus, no! You really shouldn't go!" *(Kids lower the Limbo pole. Narrator motions for others to come forward and Limbo as they shout.)*

Audience: No, Jesus, no! You really shouldn't go! No, Jesus, no! You really shouldn't go!

Narrator: But Zacchaeus said, "Wait! I'll give half of everything I have to the poor! And if I cheated any of my homies here, I'll pay back my cut and give them four times extra!" Jesus thought that was pretty cool. So he said to Zacchaeus, "You're one righteous dude!" *(Gives thumbs-up.)* Salvation came to Zacchaeus and his whole household. And all God's people said: "Whoop! Whoop!" *(Clap! Clap!)* "Whoop! Whoop!" *(Kids lower the Limbo pole. Narrator motions for others to come forward and Limbo as they shout.)*

Audience: Whoop! Whoop! *(Clap! Clap!)* Whoop! Whoop!

(REPEAT SHOUTING AND CLAPPING UNTIL YOU HAVE A LIMBO WINNER!)

How Low Can You Go, Zacchaeus?

Sticky Talk

Use these discussion points with your group following the skit.

1. Tell about a situation in which you felt like you fell short of what was expected of you. Explain whether you think the people on TV and commercials look like what we'd call "normal" people. Describe what normal is to you. Tell about a time you made up your mind about someone without getting to know him or her because of what you saw or heard about that person. What happened?

2. Think about what happens when people want to get the hottest band's concert tickets. Describe what you hear or see about the crowds. Explain whether there's any band or singer or movie you'd stand in line overnight to see and why. Explain whether you think Jesus would get the same reaction today.

3. Sometimes people can dislike someone because they don't understand that person. Sometimes people dislike others because of where they were born or what they look like. But sometimes a person is truly horrible on purpose. Incredibly, those are the kind of people Jesus decided to spend time with. Describe how hard it would be for you to forgive Zacchaeus. Talk about a time someone in your life got a second chance when that person didn't deserve it.

4. Everyone gets God's grace—whether they deserve it or not. (That's why they call it "grace.") Describe whether it's hard for you to see someone you don't like getting something he or she doesn't deserve—and why.

5. You've probably heard of "WWJD"—What Would Jesus Do? What if the letters meant "Where Would Jesus Dine?" The Pharisees were mad because of who Jesus ate lunch with. Imagine you saw Jesus having lunch with someone you knew had done really bad things. Explain whether that would change what you think about Jesus.

D.O.A.

Purpose: Lazarus' situation is retold in a modern-day, silly way. This skit emphasizes that although we may panic, God is in control and can change what we may determine to be a hopeless situation.

Passage: John 11:1-45

People: Mary, Martha, Nurse, Doctor, Jesus, Lazarus

Props:
- table
- bedsheet
- 2 cellphones (for Martha and Jesus)
- 6 copies of the skit

Prep: Choose whichever role you'd like, and then select others for the rest. Give each person a copy of the skit. Have Lazarus lie on the table. Cover him with the sheet. Have Mary and Martha stand by one side of the table and the Nurse and Doctor stand by the other side.

Note to Director: Prior to the skit, practice the medical equipment "beeps" with the kids. Cue the beeps as if you're a choir director.

Percolator

Doctor: *(Shakes head.)* Ladies, this doesn't look good. Lazarus is in pretty bad shape.

Martha: *(Places hands on chest.)* What? You said he had strep! We just need some antibiotics, right?

Doctor: I'm afraid I must've missed the diagnosis. *(Hangs head.)* I'm not sure what Lazarus has, but I'm pretty sure he's going to die.

Mary: *(Holds on to Martha.)* Die?! Sweet fancy Moses, this can't be happening! What're we going to do?

Martha: *(Pats Mary's back.)* Jesus could help!

Mary: *(Shakes head.)* Martha, I think he's awfully busy.

Martha: *(Pulls out cellphone.)* Surely Jesus can help! I'm texting him right now! *(Starts texting.)*

Mary: *(Claps hands together.)* Oh, right! Great idea!

Nurse: Well, you'd better tell your "Jesus" to get here stat! *(Holds Lazarus' wrist to check his pulse.)*

Doctor: The patient's vitals are starting to tank…*(Cues audience to sound like medical equipment—four slow beeps and then a long one.)*

Audience: Beep, beep, beep, beep, beeeeeeeeeeep.

Mary and Martha: *(Crying)* Noooo!

(DOCTOR, MARY, MARTHA, AND NURSE LEAN OVER LAZARUS, CRYING. JESUS WALKS IN BEHIND THEM.)

Jesus: Hey, did somebody text me?

(EVERYONE JUMPS, STARTLED.)

Doctor: *(Turns to Jesus.)* Jesus?!

Jesus: That's my name...*(Points finger at doctor.)* So what's all the crying about?

Martha: *(Holds up phone.)* I texted you a long time ago!

Mary: *(Wipes tears from face.)* Now it's too late!

Nurse: *(Wrings hands.)* We did everything we could. We worked on him for hours, but…

Mary and Martha: Lazarus is *dead!* *(Start crying again.)*

STiCKY BiBLe SKiTS
20 Comical Skits for Children's Ministry from the skitguys

Jesus: *(Holds hands out.)* Whoa, ladies, whoa. I got this. Everyone stand back.

(DOCTOR, NURSE, MARY, AND MARTHA MOVE AWAY FROM LAZARUS AS JESUS APPROACHES THE TABLE. JESUS HOLDS BOTH ARMS UP DRAMATICALLY TO THE SKY. THEN HE POKES LAZARUS A FEW TIMES WITH ONE FINGER.)

Jesus: *(Turns back to Mary, Martha, and medical staff.)* Well, he's dead all right. Let me see what I can do. *(Knocks two times on Lazarus' head.)* Knock, knock. *(Leans closer to Lazarus' face and knocks two more times on his head.)* I said, "Knock, knock."

Lazarus: *(Blinks eyes, opens them, and then sits up.)* Who's there?

Jesus: *(Places hand on Lazarus' shoulder.)* Laz.

Lazarus: Laz who?

Jesus: Laz time I saw you, you were dead! *(Sticks hand up to Lazarus for a high five.)*

Lazarus: *(Slaps Jesus' hand.)* All right!

Doctor: Amazing! *(Cues the audience to sound like medical equipment, beeping like crazy.)*

Audience: Beep, beep, beep, beep, beep…

Nurse: *(Runs offstage, screaming.)* Aaaah!

(MARY AND MARTHA RUN UP TO LAZARUS AND HUG HIM. EQUIPMENT STOPS BEEPING.)

Martha: Sweet fancy Moses, he's alive!

Doctor: *(Looks at ceiling.)* Thank God!

Jesus: *(Points at doctor.)* You're welcome!

Lazarus: *(Motions to everyone.)* Hey, guys! I feel like I haven't eaten in days! Who wants pizza?

Everyone: *(Raise right hand.)* I do!

Jesus: Whoa, everybody, whoa. I got this. Everybody stand back…*(Holds both arms up dramatically toward the sky and then starts poking cellphone with one finger.)*

D.O.A.

Use these discussion points with your group following the skit.

1. Prayer isn't instant messaging. Prayer isn't a wish list for Santa. Prayer *is* a conversation with God. Explain why you think we get upset if God doesn't answer our prayers with what we want when we want it. Tell about a time the answer to your prayer was "Hang on." Tell about a time the answer to your prayer was "No."

2. Why do you think God lets us feel pain? Explain whether you think God feels pain. Talk about whether you think pain helps us grow as people.

3. In the Bible, Martha tells Jesus, "If only you had been here..." Tell about a time you blamed your pain on God. Explain whether the situation was really God's fault. Tell about a time you wanted something really badly and it didn't happen. Looking at the situation now, explain whether you think it was God's fault.

4. Jesus knew what would happen with Lazarus, yet the Bible tells us "Jesus wept." What does it mean to you to know that Jesus wept even though he knew things would be okay?

5. Describe something that was a big loss in your life. Talk about how you got through that situation. When you're faced with sadness, how can you remember that Jesus is there, grieving with you?

Index

Coffee Category

Instant

Almost Instant

Percolator

Topic

Bible Passages

Sticky Bible Skits
20 Comical Skits for Children's Ministry from the skit**guys**